insight text guide

Sue Sciortino

Selected Poems

William Wordsworth

insight®

▶innovative ▶engaging ▶evolving

First published in 2008, reprinted in 2019, 2020, 2021, 2022, 2023, 2024.

Insight Publications Pty Ltd
3/350 Charman Road
Cheltenham VIC 3192
Australia
Tel: +61 3 8571 4950
Email: books@insightpublications.com.au

www.insightpublications.com.au

National Library of Australia Cataloguing-in-Publication entry:

Sciortino, Sue, 1943-
William Wordsworth's selected poems / Sue Sciortino.
1st ed.
9781921088896 (pbk.)
Insight text guide.
Bibliography.
For secondary school age.
Wordsworth, William, 1770-1850 --Poetic works.
Wordsworth, William, 1770-1850 --Criticism and interpretation.
821.7

Other ISBNs:
9781925778830 (digital)

Cover design by Gisela Beer, based on a concept by The Modern Art Production Group

Proudly Printed in Australia by Ligare Book Printers.

contents

NARRATIVE VOICES, IMAGERY & THEMES

Narrative voice	**Effect**	**Key poems**
First-person	Intimately engages the reader; used in many poems as the poet/ speaker	'Lines Written in Early Spring' 'Michael' 'Ode: Intimations of Immortality' 'Resolution and Independence'
Complex first-person	Gives depth to the poetic account	'The Ruined Cottage'
Imagery	**Effect**	**Key poems**
Nature	Explores deeper meaning of existence	'I Wandered Lonely as a Cloud' 'Tintern Abbey' *The Prelude* Books I and II 'Yew-Trees'
Man's work in nature	Shows technology and architecture essential to human activity	'Composed Upon Westminster Bridge' 'Steamboats, Viaducts, and Railways'
Images of rustics	Poet teaches through simplicity	'Resolution and Independence' 'The Solitary Reaper'
Themes	**Ideas conveyed**	**Key poems**
Wisdom of childhood	Sees childish innocence as source of great wisdom	'It is a beauteous Evening' 'My heart leaps up' 'We Are Seven' 'Ode: Intimations of Immortality'
Family & community	Shows dislocation in society	'Michael'
Loss	Explores importance of relationships	'Lucy Gray' 'The Ruined Cottage'
Irrational fear & death	Shows how experiences of fear and visions of death can inspire dignity and awe	'Strange Fits of Passion' 'A slumber did my spirit steal' *The Prelude* Book I

POEMS ANALYSED IN THIS GUIDE

This guide uses the Penguin Classics *Selected Poems* (ed. Stephen Gill, 2004) as its primary source. However, the versions of the poems selected in this edition often vary from more accepted versions; for two short poems, 'I Wandered Lonely as a Cloud' and 'Strange Fits of Passion Have I Known', these differences are so significant that the preferred versions are provided in the Appendix for easy reference. Moreover, some important poems are not included in the *Selected Poems*. I recommend *The Norton Anthology of English Literature, Vol. II* (Abrams 1979) as an additional reference and source. It is important to note the differences, especially in *The Prelude*, since the *Norton Anthology* provides Wordsworth's final revised version (1839), whereas the excerpts in the *Selected Poems* are from the earliest complete version (1805).

The following poems from the *Selected Poems* are analysed in detail in this guide:

'A slumber did my spirit seal'
'Composed Upon Westminster Bridge'
'I Wandered Lonely as a Cloud' (also known as 'Daffodils'; see the Appendix for the version analysed in this guide)
'It is a beauteous Evening'
'Lines Written a Few Miles above Tintern Abbey' (usually known simply as 'Tintern Abbey')
'Lines Written in Early Spring'
'Lucy Gray'
'Michael'
'My heart leaps up'
'Nutting'
'Ode: Intimations of Immortality'
'Resolution and Independence'
'Strange fits of passion I have known' (see the Appendix for the version analysed in this guide)

The Prelude

'The Ruined Cottage'

'The Solitary Reaper'

'We Are Seven'

'Yew-Trees'

'Steamboats, Viaducts, and Railways' is also discussed, although it is not included in the *Selected Poems* – see the Appendix for this poem.

Further poems referred to are:

'A Night-Piece'

'A Whirl-Blast from Behind the Hill' (not in the *Selected Poems* – see *The Norton Anthology of English Literature, Vol. II*)

'Gipsies'

'She dwelt among th' untrodden ways'

'Surprized by joy'

'The Thorn'

'The Two April Mornings'

'Three years she grew in sun and shower'

OVERVIEW

About William Wordsworth (1770–1850)

William Wordsworth was born on 7 April 1770 at Cockermouth on the River Derwent, at about the same time as Captain Cook first sighted the east coast of Australia and expanded the reach of the British Empire. Wordsworth's birthplace, in the heart of the Lake District of England, would later come to be immortalised in his poetry.

The son of a prominent lawyer, John Wordsworth, William was the second of five children. William's father was the personal attorney of the Earl of Lonsdale, the most powerful man in the area. Because John Wordsworth was a professional, William was given the advantage of a formal education at Anne Birkett's school at Penrith. He met his future wife, Mary Hutchinson, while studying there.

Wordsworth's mother's death in 1778 led to the disintegration of the family, as William and his three brothers were sent to Hawkshead Grammar School. William quickly settled into this new environment, regarding it as his true home, especially after his father died in 1783. It was an excellent school, providing William with a solid foundation in the classics, mathematics and science.

William was heavily influenced by those around him in this period. His young headmaster, William Taylor, encouraged his fledgling attempts to write poetry. Taylor is celebrated in the persona of Matthew in 'The Two April Mornings' (pp.68–70). Ann Tyson, the woman with whom the Wordsworth boys boarded, was also a major influence on the young poet. She became, in effect, a surrogate mother and provided William with the structured family life he craved; crucially for his later work, she also allowed him the freedom to explore the natural beauty of the Lake District. Ann Tyson is immortalised as the 'frugal dame' in the poem 'Nutting' (pp.75–6).

When William's father died, he was owed a small fortune by the Earl of Lonsdale – a debt Lonsdale avoided paying until 1802. Despite Lonsdale's reticence, William's uncles took financial responsibility for him, enabling him to matriculate at Cambridge in 1787 although he lacked interest in academic honours.

Wordsworth rejected the path that his relatives and mentors expected of him. Declining the proposed careers of clergyman or lawyer, William tried to educate himself in other, less academic ways. In the summer of 1790 he went on a walking tour of Europe, and arrived in France in time for the celebration of the first year of the French Revolution.

The impact of this visit on the impressionable young man was far-reaching. Returning to France in November of 1791 as an ardent supporter of the French Revolution, Wordsworth fell in love with Annette Vallon, who bore him a daughter. Although William may have intended to marry her, money problems forced him to return home just as war broke out between England and France. William did not return to France until 1802.

In 1795 Wordsworth inherited a small income from a young friend who died of tuberculosis, finally allowing him to devote himself to poetry. He met Samuel Taylor Coleridge in August of that year and the two young poets quickly became close friends.

In 1797 William and his sister, Dorothy, moved near Coleridge in the Lake District where the friends embarked on an intensely creative period that resulted, in 1798, in the first edition of *Lyrical Ballads*, their first published work. This volume, which included both Coleridge's 'The Ancient Mariner' and Wordsworth's 'Lines Written a Few Miles above Tintern Abbey', plainly signalled a new literary movement. Wordsworth acknowledged that he drew inspiration for his poems in *Lyrical Ballads* from his sister Dorothy, whose imaginative observations of nature and tender disposition provided the spark for many of his poems. She is described in 'Tintern Abbey' as 'my dearest Friend' and 'My dear, dear Sister' (p.65).

In 1800 a second edition was published, including the famous 'Preface' planned in close consultation with Coleridge that explained the rationale behind the new poetry. This edition bore only Wordsworth's name, after the first edition had been published anonymously. Although the two friends later had a falling out, a third edition was published in 1802 – the year that Wordsworth became financially independent after the death of the Earl of Lonsdale.

1802 was a landmark year for Wordsworth in several other ways. Nine years of war between France and England ended with the Peace of Amiens, which allowed William to finally meet his daughter, Caroline; he provided her with an allowance for the rest of her life. It was also the year that he married Mary Hutchinson. The turn of the nineteenth century was an extremely dynamic time creatively for Wordsworth, and he produced most of his best poems during this time.

Wordsworth's youthful idealism was not to last. After this brief period of happiness, he was beset by hardships and frustrations. His disillusionment with the violent course that the French Revolution took was completed when Napoleon crowned himself Emperor in 1804; as a result, Wordsworth became more politically conservative. Adding to Wordsworth's distress was the death by drowning of his younger sailor brother, John, who died captaining his ship in 1805.

Yet 1805 was also the year that he completed his greatest work, *The Prelude*. His financial stability was ensured when he received the post of Stamp Distributor (that is, revenue collector) for Westmoreland. While this government position was certainly lucrative, it led to accusations by later writers that he was a political turncoat who had betrayed his earlier radicalism.

Wordsworth died as a well-respected Poet Laureate in 1850, a post that he had held since 1843. He was still considered the greatest poet in the world by many, although his work after 1807 had made little impact on either the critics or the public. *The Prelude*, a long autobiographical work that he continued to revise almost to the end, was published after his death.

Wordsworth's divided loyalties between England and France, his gradual disillusionment with the course of the French Revolution and his feelings of guilt over Annette Vallon all combined to bring him to the brink of an emotional breakdown. The process of working through and overcoming these dilemmas underpins many of Wordsworth's greatest poems. But the great elegiac voice that he had established in the early dirges to Lucy did not last, as his early emotional experiences could not continue to provide an inexhaustible resource for poetry.

Introduction to Wordsworth's poetry

William Wordsworth was a prominent member of the group of poets later dubbed 'Romantics'. Breaking with earlier established views of the way poetry should be written, he believed that the poet's role was to guide others through the transforming power of the poetic imagination.

As set out in his 'Preface' to *Lyrical Ballads* in 1800 and 1802 (Abrams 1979), he held that a poet must be trained in the use of the senses and the imagination to respond spontaneously to experiences which may be meaningless to others. His decision to use 'common' language in his poetry was designed to enhance communication between poet and audience, as well as signalling his refusal to be restricted by established conventions of poetic expression. Seeking to breathe imaginative life into all human experiences, Wordsworth spoke to everyday men and women on their own level, as well as being able to converse with other poets as a contemporary and equal. To this end, he often assumed the persona and voice of a poet-prophet in his work. However, the private person always comes through in his poetry, because the experiences he relates are verifiably his own.

Because Wordsworth's imagination was often sparked by a simple encounter or experience, he deduced that the profoundest elements of human knowledge can be gained from the simplest principles of nature. Despite this focus on the natural world, Wordsworth's meditative outlook means that he cannot be dismissed as a mere 'nature' poet. The natural scene constitutes the organising principle of the poem, but for Wordsworth the 'Mind of Man' is the vital element that apprehends and captures the natural world in poetry.

In 'Romantic' poetry, the source of poetry was located in the individual poet rather than the external world. In a dramatic reversal of the biblical promise of divine redemption, which claimed that hope was only administered by God, the Romantics put forward an idea of hope that was centred in humanity. The Romantics' God, then, becomes an *active* power within the natural world, rather than a distant authority. The poet, as interpreter of nature, assumes the role of producing the moral improvement of his fellow men and helping them to make sense of their transient existence. Wordsworth challenges his readers to look at life differently through the power of the poetic imagination, in order to show that each person must create their own system of meaning by which to live.

BACKGROUND & CONTEXT

Historical and political context

Wordsworth lived at a time of great political and social change in England and throughout Europe. Two of the most important events that had a significant impact on his poetry – as well as on his overall outlook and values – were the Industrial Revolution and the French Revolution.

Industrial Revolution (1750–1800s)

The shift in methods of manufacturing that resulted from the invention of power-driven machinery to replace hand labour is commonly called the 'Industrial Revolution'. After centuries of almost imperceptibly slow change, economic and social conditions in the Western world began a rapid, industry-generated transformation. This massive, often painful upheaval had a profound impact on Wordsworth's society, not least environmentally. Improvements in technology made the production of goods far more efficient and cost effective, leading to the establishment of the first factories, particularly for the manufacture of textiles.

The rise of the factory permanently altered the English landscape. As mechanisation increased, labouring workers massed in the sprawling mill towns to find employment. In central and northern England, towns such as Leeds and Manchester grew quickly, a rate of growth largely made possible by James Watt's development of the steam engine in 1765.

Rural communities were doubly affected. Firstly, they lost their home industries to large manufacturers. Secondly, there was a rapid increase in the process of 'enclosure' – the method of enclosing open fields and communally worked farms into privately owned agricultural holdings. Supplying the quickly growing population required the development of more efficient methods of agriculture and animal breeding, techniques which worked best on large, privately owned farms. People were forced either to join the manufacturing labourers or to remain on starvation wages as subsistence farmers, creating a new 'landless class'.

The factories' vast appetite for coal led to the establishment of a network of coalmines, in which labourers experienced the harshest working conditions of all: children as young as five were harnessed to heavy coal-sledges, which they dragged by crawling on their hands and knees. However, such suffering was largely confined to the poor; in stark contrast to this terrible poverty, the 'leisure class' in London indulged in lavish displays of wealth and moral laxity.

As a result of these rapid changes, the population was polarised into the two classes of 'capital' and 'labour'. The former class consisted of factory owners and traders (the rich); the latter of possessionless wage earners (the poor).

Both Wordsworth and Coleridge became increasingly hostile to industrialisation, seeking to immortalise the lost rural landscape in their poetry. The Romantic focus on the natural world can be seen as a passionate reaction against the Industrial Revolution and its corrosive effects on the individual, the community and the landscape.

French Revolution

In Paris on 14 July 1789, French rebels stormed the Bastille, the ultimate symbol of tyranny and feudalism. Led by the disenfranchised (without the right to vote) middle classes, the rebels' demands were simple but profound: abolition of class privilege, including that of the dominant clergy; equitable taxation; reform of the law, particularly in regard to crimes against the Church that were punishable by death, such as sacrilege; and universal human rights.

The principles of liberty, fraternity and equality that underpinned the French Revolution appealed strongly to Wordsworth, for a revolutionary energy was also at the core of Romanticism. In England, though, France was an object of fear and loathing. This was largely due to the threat of invasion, both on a literal level and on the level of ideas. In addition, the principles of the Revolution challenged every monarchy in Europe, including England's.

By 1793 the French Revolution had become more extreme, placing pressure on Wordsworth's initial support. Under threat from a variety of groups, the revolutionaries gradually became more violent and extreme. A bloody 'Reign of Terror', as it has since become known, ensued, particularly after the execution of King Louis XVI in that year.

Wordsworth was affected in a very personal way by the Revolution and subsequent wars between Britain and France. He spent much of 1792 in France observing the Revolution, and had an affair with Annette Vallon who gave birth to his child. In 1793 the onset of war between England and France made it impossible for him to return to France, a situation which led to personal turmoil. Wordsworth was torn between his allegiances to the two countries. Additionally, his life was quite possibly under threat in England, because his radical politics were seen as too closely aligned with the French.

Wordsworth gradually grew disenchanted with the Revolution. Abolition of class privilege – one of the main demands of the French people in 1789 – was one of the volatile issues that Wordsworth sought to address in England, but his early enthusiasm for the French Revolution changed when he saw its ideals corrupted.

Tormented at seeing his political principles betrayed by the Reign of Terror, and filled with remorse and love for Annette Vallon, this post-Revolutionary period was one of the most difficult of Wordsworth's life.

Feminism

In Wordsworth's England, women constituted a universally deprived class. Widely regarded as inferior to men in intellect and in all but domestic talents, they were provided with limited schooling and had no access to higher education. Only menial vocations were open to them, and they possessed few legal rights. The few rights they did possess were further reduced after marriage, when husbands maintained supreme authority, even over a woman's inheritance.

This began to change when women acquired a strong and eloquent champion in Mary Wollstonecraft. In 1792 she wrote the founding classic of the feminist movement, *A Vindication of the Rights of Woman*, asserting that women possess equal intellectual capacity and talents to men. This book was unprecedented in its firsthand observations of the inequities and indignities suffered by women, and in the passion with which it exposed and decried such injustice. This was also the first sociological treatise that demonstrated how the oppression of women distorts the social process by warping men's values and behaviour – in other words, irresponsibly wielded power corrupts both the oppressor and the oppressed. Wollstonecraft demanded greater equality of social, educational and vocational privileges but, despite her efforts, the cause of women's rights was not taken up effectively until much later, in the nineteenth and twentieth centuries.

Women had little chance of improving their lot without major reforms to England's exploitative class system. Gradually, however, working-class reformers acquired the support of the middle classes and the liberal thinkers in government. Finally, the acute economic distress of the working classes was recognised and, after intense agitation and protest that threatened to break into revolution, the first Reform Bill was carried in 1832 at the end of the Romantic period. Although the reforms were mild by today's standards, parliamentary representation and the right to vote was extended to men who did not own land. The principle of peaceful adjustment of conflicting interests by Parliamentary majority had been firmly established, and a process for reform recognised.

The reforms were imperfect and incomplete, however. About half the middle class, almost all the working class and all women remained disenfranchised. Although Queen Victoria, the most powerful woman in the world at that time, acceded to the throne in 1832, women only achieved a vote in England in the 1930s. This right was won much earlier in New Zealand (1893) and Australia (South Australia allowed women to vote from 1894, for example).

Wordsworth was in many ways sympathetic to the women's movement. His obvious fondness for, and lifelong protection of, his sister Dorothy strongly suggests that he was sympathetic towards women – although he did not overtly advocate an improvement in women's rights. Throughout his poems, though, he treats women with empathy and even reverence, such as the character of Isobel in 'Michael' (pp.114–27) and the lone female figure in 'The Solitary Reaper' (pp.165–6).

Literary context

Romanticism 1798–1832

Romanticism has little to do with the popular concept of 'romantic' love. Rather, it was an artistic and philosophical movement that redefined the fundamental ways in which people in Western cultures thought about themselves and their world.

The term 'Romanticism' was coined after the Romantic period, in the second half of the nineteenth century, to refer to a revolutionary approach to the creative arts, particularly in painting, music and literature.

The poets classed as 'Romantics' rejected the classical forms that they inherited from their eighteenth-century predecessors, such as Pope and Dryden. These 'neo-classicists' (so called because they used the classical models of ancient Greek and Roman writers) wrote on grand subjects that were regarded as the only suitable material for the poetic arts. Writing in established, highly structured literary forms, the neo-classicists' poetry reflected a shared desire for an ordered, civilsed society. They were financially supported by rich patrons who largely governed their subject matter.

In contrast to their conservative forebears, the Romantic poets were often radical, both politically and in their choice of literary forms; and they typically wrote about rural rather than urban environments. They developed an aesthetic freedom from formal rules and poetic conventions in order to achieve a high level of genuine self-expression and to convey intense emotions in their work. Because they usually had to provide their own income to sustain their art, they had more freedom to choose their subject matter.

Despite these common elements, Romanticism was not a unified movement with a clearly defined literary or political agenda. The Romantic poets did share certain concerns, but their attitudes often differed on personal, religious and political levels.

Key point

Wordsworth's definition of all good poetry as 'the spontaneous overflow of powerful feelings' (in the 'Preface' to *Lyrical Ballads*) marks a turning point in literary history. By locating the ultimate source of poetry in the individual artist, the Romantics reversed the tradition, stretching back to the ancients, of valuing art primarily for its ability to imitate human life (that is, for its mimetic qualities). Romantic poets valued art not as a mirror of the external world, but as a means of illuminating the world within the poet's soul.

The revolutionary energy underlying Romanticism affected not just literature, but all of the arts – music (particularly Romantic opera), painting, sculpture and architecture. The movement rapidly spread to other Western societies, including the New World countries of the United States and Australia.

Who were the Romantic poets?

As there was an early and a late Romantic period, the poets can be separated into first and second generations. The major poets of the first generation are:

- William Blake (1757–1827)
- William Wordsworth (1770–1850)
- Samuel Taylor Coleridge (1772–1834).

The second generation's major poets are:

- George Gordon, Lord Byron (1788–1824)
- Percy Bysshe Shelley (1792–1822)
- John Keats (1795–1821).

Shaped by the events of an earlier period, Wordsworth and his close associate Coleridge can be seen as groundbreakers of the Romantic movement in poetry.

The influence of Rousseau (1712–1778)

Jean-Jacques Rousseau, a French philosopher and novelist, influenced English Romantics such as Wordsworth. Rousseau had rebelled against rigid social conventions and excessive formality in the arts, arguing instead for the primacy of feeling and imagination over law, convention and reason. He believed that humans could become morally ennobled by returning to nature and liberating themselves from the artificial constraints imposed by society. His view of human nature was fundamentally optimistic, proposing that society and its institutions, in particular its laws, had corrupted humanity from a state of natural innocence. In 1762 Rousseau's *The Social Contract* was published, introducing the phrase 'liberty, equality, fraternity' which was so influential on early revolutionary thinkers.

The eighteenth-century cult of the 'noble savage', which resulted from Rousseau's concepts, promoted similar ideals to those adopted by the Romantics. They turned to domestic rather than exotic sources for inspiration, using folk legends and older, less sophisticated art forms, such as the ballad; their characters were often contemporary country folk who spoke the language of common people, rather than a stilted and artificial poetic diction.

The role of the imagination

Wordsworth and his fellow Romantics saw the imagination as the supreme faculty of the human mind, contrasting sharply with traditional arguments for the supremacy of reason. The Romantics defined the imagination as the ultimate shaping, or creative, power. They saw it as dynamic, active rather than passive, and containing the primary energy for creating all art. The imagination also helps us to *constitute* reality: as Wordsworth suggested, we not only perceive, but also partly create, the world around us. Uniting reason and feeling, the imagination is extolled as the ultimate synthesising capability, enabling us to reconcile differences in the world of appearance. It is this new focus on the role of the imagination, and faith in its transformative powers, that so starkly separates the Romantics from their predecessors.

STRUCTURE, STYLE & LANGUAGE

In his 'Preface' to *Lyrical Ballads* published in 1802 (see Abrams 1979), Wordsworth set out a revolutionary new theory of poetry, based on the premise that 'all good poetry is the spontaneous overflow of powerful feelings'. By this he meant that, even though the creative process is influenced by the poet's prior thoughts and poetic skill, the composition must reflect the spontaneity of the original experience. He did not mean that the actual diction of his rustics, peasants, children and outcasts should be recorded in their own dialects but, instead, that he was using a 'selection of language really used by men' rather than the elevated poetic diction that was used in pre-Romantic poetry:

> I have proposed to myself to imitate and, as far as is possible, to adopt the very language of men ... I have at all times endeavoured to look steadily at my subject; consequently, I hope that there is in these poems little falsehood of description, and that my ideas are expressed in language fitted to their respective importance.

Viewing poetry as being 'the image of man and nature', Wordsworth here considers humankind and nature as being essentially adapted to each other, and the human mind as a natural mirror of the fairest and most interesting qualities of nature.

Examining Wordsworth's poetry, then, will allow us to explore whether Wordsworth is successful in presenting humans in nature as he proposed in his 'Preface'.

Poetic diction and devices

Poetic language is generally more intensive and figurative than that of everyday speech and prose (novels and short stories). The term 'poetic diction' refers to a poet's personal language, including the words, phrases and poetic devices that are not used in ordinary speech.

Poetic diction changes through time. At various periods in literature, poets have used 'elevated' language to convey beauty and/or nobility of thought. At other times, especially in the twentieth century, poets constantly trialled new approaches to capture the immediacy of lived experience and so the 'poetic language' we read today has become much more varied and fluid than it often had been in the past.

In order to analyse poetic diction, you need to know and understand the most commonly used poetic techniques or devices. These are listed with brief definitions below. (For more detailed definitions, see a reputable dictionary of literary terms, e.g. Abrams 1971.)

1 Establish the **persona** – the person speaking in the poem. (See the notes in the 'Narrative voice' section of this guide, pages 37–43). The word *persona* comes from Latin meaning 'mask' and originally applied to drama. In poetry, the persona is often the first-person narrator of a poem.

2 How does the poem's **form** contribute to the reader's understanding of what the poem is about?
   - Is it a strictly rhyming poem?
   - Are the verses of even length?
   - Is the poem in free verse?
   - Why do different poets use different poetic forms?

   Wordsworth's poems vary from blank verse to lyrics to highly patterned stanza forms. They include:
   - epic poems such as *The Prelude*
   - long narratives such as 'Michael' and 'The Ruined Cottage'
   - sonnets (Petrarchan rather than Shakespearean in form) such as 'It is a beauteous Evening'
   - lyrics such as 'I Wandered Lonely as a Cloud'
   - odes: the formal eighteenth-century form of the ode is addressed to a personified abstraction, such as in 'Ode: Intimations of Immortality'.

3 Does the **rhythm** (metre) evoke an emotional response?

4 How does the **rhyme** scheme help to make the poem effective? Wordsworth uses a variety of rhyme schemes:

- Blank verse (unrhymed, ten-syllable lines) in long poems, such as *The Prelude*, 'Resolution and Independence', 'Michael' and 'The Ruined Cottage'.
- Strict rhyming stanzas in lyrics, such as 'I Wandered Lonely as a Cloud'. In this poem the six-line stanzas have four lines of alternate rhyme, ending with a rhyming couplet.
- Fourteen-line sonnets, such as 'Composed Upon Westminster Bridge', with an *abba abba* rhyme scheme in the octave (first eight lines); and a *cdcdcd* rhyme scheme in the sestet (final six lines).
- The simple *abab* rhyme scheme of poems such as 'We Are Seven' is used to support the balladic form.
- Rhyming couplets, such as in 'Gipsies', create a rollicking rhythm.

5 What kind of **vocabulary** is used?
- Is the poem packed with adjectives and adverbs?
- Is it purely descriptive?
- How are contrasting words used for effect?

6 What kind of **emotional response** does the language elicit?
- Does it make the reader feel sad/happy/angry etc.?
- Is the reader's sympathy engaged?

7 What kind of **tone** does the poet use? Tone implies a speaker, and refers to the attitude of the poet towards the reader and/or subject matter. To identify the tone (which can change within a poem), read the poem aloud.
- Is the tone solemn, joyful, serious, ironic, sad?
- Is there a reliance on irony, wit, persuasion etc. to win over the reader?

8 Is the **voice** used in the poem private or public? Is it one of:
- a storyteller
- a commentator
- a reporter
- a bystander
- an observer
- a person reflecting in private?

9 What **devices** does the poet employ to manipulate the reader's response? See the table below for a summary of poetic devices and examples in Wordsworth's poetry.

10 What kinds of **images** promote an understanding of what the poet is trying to convey?

11 What makes the poem memorable?

Device	Definition	Wordsworth examples
Simile	comparison using 'as' or 'like' to create an image or meaning	• 'my Boat/Went heaving through the water, *like* a Swan' (*The Prelude* Bk.1, ll.403–4) • 'Motionless *as* a Cloud' ('Resolution and Independence', l.82) • '*like* an untired horse' (*The Prelude* Bk.1, l.459) • '*like* a book preserved the memory/Of the dumb animals' ('Michael', ll.70–1) • 'Tinkled *like* iron' (*The Prelude* Bk.1, l.469); this is also onomatopoeic (sound of the word echoing the sound it denotes)
Metaphor	a comparison in which one thing is described as another	• 'The clear Moon ... There, in a black-blue vault she sails along' ('A Night-Piece', ll.13–14) • 'all those leaves, in festive glee/Were dancing to the minstrelsy' ('A Whirl-Blast from Behind the Hill', ll.21–2) • 'a huge Cliff ... Upreared its head' (*The Prelude* Bk.1, ll.406–8)
Alliteration	repetition of consonants for emphasis	• 'weary weight' ('Tintern Abbey', l.40) • 'hunted hare' (*The Prelude* Bk.1, l.464) • 'And in the frosty season, when the sun/Was set' (*The Prelude* Bk.1, ll.452–3); repetition of 's'
Assonance	repetition of vowel ('a', 'e', 'i', 'o', 'u') sounds	• 'I wandered lonely as a cloud/That floats on High o'er vales and hills/When all at once I saw a crowd/A host of golden daffodils' ('I Wandered Lonely as a Cloud', ll.1–4) • 'The cock is crowing/The stream is flowing' ('Written in March', ll.1–2)
Personification	giving human attributes to an inanimate object	• 'golden daffodils ... dancing in the breeze ... Tossing their heads in sprightly dance' ('I Wandered Lonely as a Cloud', ll.4–12)
Onomatopoeia	sound imitating sense	• 'The small birds twitter' ('Written in March', l.3) • 'We hissed along the polished ice' (*The Prelude* Bk.1, l.461)

Wordsworth's use of imagery

One way of approaching a response to Wordsworth's poetry is through a careful explication of the imagery he uses both to dramatise narratives and to present his view of nature and our place within the natural world. Nature is the element that imbues his work with a spiritual dimension, as he places either himself (as the speaker/poet) or another character in an environment that will teach that speaker or character to understand their place within the complete cycle from birth to death.

Images work in complex ways. A poem's meaning can operate on several levels at the same time, an effect which can be achieved through a layering of images and ambiguity. To achieve his desired effects, Wordsworth uses a range of poetic devices, such as metaphor and simile, and is most successful when he uses concrete rather than abstract images.

Key point

Above all, Wordsworth seeks to convey his view that it is the capacity to meditate on nature that allows us to achieve an understanding of the completeness of the universe in which we live. Through a series of multifaceted images, Wordsworth leads us to a better understanding of our own lives as we, too, reflect upon our surroundings. The poet uses his imagination to create his world. As we read, we not only re-create his poems, but are guided to fashion our own world through the medium of our individual imaginations. That is his ultimate purpose.

Images of nature

Wordsworth is often categorised as a poet of nature, although it is the individual in nature that is the true focus of his poetry. This can be seen even in poems that seem deceptively simple, such as **'I Wandered Lonely as a Cloud'** (often better known as 'Daffodils'; see the Appendix for the version of this poem analysed here). In this poem, Wordsworth captures a remembered experience 'in tranquillity'. The natural world is utilised as a tool to explore the deeper meaning of human existence, a goal that Wordsworth achieves by meditating on his earlier experiences.

In this poem, dated 1804, Wordsworth's imagination reorders an earlier experience from 1802, demonstrating the method he outlines in his 'Preface'. The first stanza conveys the speaker's first sight of a mass display of daffodils. It begins with a simile likening the speaker's wandering to that of a 'cloud' floating (l.1). He is startled in his country walk by the sight of 'a crowd' (l.3) of 'golden daffodils' (l.4). The word 'host' (l.4) qualifies 'crowd', elevating the moment of first sight to a spiritual one, as the word has religious connotations that suggest angels or divinity, while 'crowd' is human. Further, the daffodils become personified in the concluding couplet of the stanza as the wind animates them into 'Fluttering and dancing' (l.6) beings. Although the daffodils are active, the speaker remains an observer only and takes no part in the scene.

Again, the second stanza begins with a simile: 'Continuous *as* the stars that shine' (l.7). This device does not suggest that the flowers are physically everlasting, but rather that they are continuous in the speaker's own mind *in his recollection*. The references to the heavens reinforce the image of this particular glimpse of nature as part of the universal order of things. The 'never-ending line' (l.9) refers back to 'Continuous', underlining the enduring impact that this image has had on the speaker. Similar to the last line of the first stanza, the daffodils are moving harmoniously, in a dance that is both an imitation of human behaviour and also a purely natural process; the speaker is merely an observer of this wonder.

In the third stanza, however, the speaker as the 'poet' becomes central; his involvement is crucial to the working of the poem. This stanza evokes what the vision of daffodils means 'to me' (l.18) – that is, the 'wealth' of nature, the theatrical moment that is available to him alone, forever in his memory. The repetition of 'gazed – and gazed' (l.17) underlines the lasting impression of this memory.

This idea becomes more overt in the last stanza where the vision in recollection, the 'flash upon that inward eye' (l.21), provides an intellectual continuity for the poet whenever he is 'pensive' (l.20), making his 'solitude' (l.22) pleasurable. His power of remembrance combined with his imagination can take him back to the marvellous moment when he danced 'with the daffodils' (l.24).

This is not a simple poem, but an intelligent and subtle account of the creative process itself and a celebration of the power of the human cognitive ability to remember and give meaning to our experiences.

Q Examine Wordsworth's use of adjectives in this poem. Refer particularly to the effects and impact of 'sprightly', 'jocund' and 'pensive'.

Q How do the verbs 'fluttering' and 'tossing' add to the movement of the poem?

Q What other words in the poem give the impression of activity?

In **'Lines Written a Few Miles above Tintern Abbey'** (pp.61–6), Wordsworth puts forward his belief that nature's ultimate role in our lives is as a teacher. Children brought up close to nature, he believed, were more sensitive and open to an appreciation of art, especially poetry. Further, nature is the teacher, 'by beauty and by fear' (*The Prelude*, Bk 1, l.306), of moral values: in 'Tintern Abbey' he proclaims that nature is 'The anchor of my purest thoughts, the nurse/The guide, the guardian of my heart, and soul/Of all my moral being' (ll.110–11).

This poem pre-empts Wordsworth's mature achievement in *The Prelude*, where he sets out the full extent of his relationship with nature and the growth of the poet's mind. 'Tintern Abbey' is important as a poem of transition between those that revel in a sensuous expression of nature, such as 'I Wandered Lonely as a Cloud', and the meditative poems, such as 'Ode: Intimations of Immortality', which are essentially philosophical explorations and celebrations of our place in the universe.

Wordsworth first visited the Wye valley and the ruins of Tintern Abbey on a walking tour in 1793. On this second occasion, 'five summers' (l.1) later, he is with his sister, Dorothy, and the evocation of his previous visit triggers a fresh appreciation of the forms and colours of the area.

Key point

In this poem Wordsworth's real subject is the development of his love of nature as he reviews his past, evaluates the present and anticipates the future.

He begins by describing the scene that inspires the speaker (with no pretence that 'I' is anyone other than Wordsworth here) – the river whose waters roll 'from their mountain-springs/With a sweet inland murmur' (ll.3–4), the 'steep and lofty cliffs' (l.5). The inspiring scene, rather than being overtly dramatic, is a landscape of serenity where the land and sky meet 'quiet[ly]' (l.8). Although the narrator communicates his sense of happiness at being back at the scene, the setting is more a frame or background for the true subject of the poem – the feelings and sensations experienced by the poet. The real significance of the landscape soon becomes apparent, for 'oft, in lonely rooms, and mid the din/Of towns and cities, I have owed to [this remembered scene] ... sensations sweet' (ll.26–9). Just as in 'I Wandered Lonely as a Cloud', the 'inward eye' of memory provides the speaker with relief in the midst of discord.

Lines 36–42 expand on this point, first building up a sense of a grave burden with their slow movement, their ponderous repetition of the awkward phrase 'In which' and the dragging, encumbering effect of alliterative phrases like 'weary weight', as if the narrator has been bowed down by contemplating the inherent sadness of the human condition. However, the tone suddenly lifts with 'Is lightened' (l.42), as a moment of illumination is reached. The lines move more freely and gently from this point. The conjunction 'Until' (l.44) begins a long clause that slowly unwinds, gradually slowing the verse down to a virtual standstill at the word 'suspended' (l.46). Then, 'we are laid asleep/In body' (ll.46–7) encapsulates the mystical state that the verse itself has achieved. With the body spellbound, the sudden energy of 'become a living soul/While with an eye made quiet by the power/Of harmony, and the deep power of joy' (ll.47–9) heralds the liberation of the mind's faculties to the state of insightful lucidity recorded in 'We see into the life of things' (l.50).

The review of his past is completed with the beautiful lines 50–8, as the speaker sums up the significance of his memory of the 'sylvan Wye' (l.57). He has found respite amidst the 'fretful stir' (l.53) and 'fever of the world' (l.54). This is not merely a recollection of a place visited, as the narrator implies that his very spirit has been nourished with his thoughts of the Wye countryside. As Wordsworth re-enacts the sequence of remembering, and vividly reliving, a past experience, we can follow the process that facilitates the speaker's state of enlightenment.

Revisiting a beloved place also affects the poet's future state of mind, as this second visit has provided 'life and food/For future years' (ll.65–6). The speaker tells us (lines 59–85) that his appreciation of the scene was incomplete on his previous visit, as his initial response was passionate, unintellectual, merely an 'appetite' – a boy's purely physical response.

But the narrator has grown out of this youthful attitude to the landscape, just as he might have responded to an early love affair, 'a feeling and a love/That had no need of a remoter charm' (ll.81–2). Now, though, 'That time is past/And all its aching joys are now no more/And all its dizzy raptures' (ll.84–6). These lines describe the melancholy process of surrendering the post-adolescent's aching, giddy passions to a more mature state of mind. He does not regret this passing, though, for 'other gifts/Have followed' (ll.87–8). Yet this is qualified by the phrase 'I would believe' (l.88), emphasising the difficulty in accepting such a loss.

This is a remarkable chronicle of a person's emotional development. But the speaker's sense of loss is carried forward, giving the lines that follow a special poignancy:

> For I have learned
> To look on nature, not as in the hour
> Of thoughtless youth; but hearing oftentimes
> The still, sad music of humanity ... (ll.89–92)

These lines, which are among Wordsworth's most beautiful, are central to the philosophical argument of the poem. The speaker claims he has learned to add thought to sensual experience for the first time. He is humbled by his painfully acquired knowledge of human suffering, even as it enriches the visible scene before him like a musical chord. Consistent with Wordsworth's belief in the importance of nature, this knowledge has the capacity to teach as well as to show. The passage also has religious overtones, as the greater 'presence' (l.95) that he now recognises links his mind with all elements of the external world.

The speaker elaborates on the capacity of this 'sense sublime' (l.96) to enrich the natural world. After inanimate nature has been shown to be fused with human nature, the connection between the two concepts is further elaborated. Here the grammatical structure adds weight to the point, as the lines are extended sonorously through the repetition of 'And' into one long sentence, from 'And I have felt' (l.94) to 'And rolls through all things' (l.103). Again, the speaker perceives a unity between the cerebral (mental) and material worlds. This is followed by the belief that imbues all of Wordsworth's poetry: that we 'half-create' (l.107) the world through our imagination. Further, the speaker's love of nature is the same as on his earlier visit, but his acquired knowledge has made it 'The anchor of [his] purest thoughts' (l.110) and, ultimately, 'The guide' (l.111) of his 'moral being' (l.112). Wordsworth thus attributes to nature the roles of teacher, moral guide and artistic creator.

The last section of the poem, anticipating the future, pays tribute to Wordsworth's sister Dorothy, his 'dear, dear Friend' (l.117) to whom he ascribes his new insight into the marriage between man and nature. 'And in after years' (l.138) looks forward to a time when brother and sister will remember the present moment and the significance of what 'this green pastoral landscape' (l.159) of the Wye valley has meant to them.

This poem marks a turning point in the development of Wordsworth's poetry because it foreshadows the contemplative direction his mature work will take.

- Compared to the earlier poem 'I Wandered Lonely as a Cloud', there is an absence of pretty images of nature.
- The language and rhythm of 'Tintern Abbey' are measured.
- The poetic sentences are longer and carry a weightier message.
- The light movement, such as the image of the daffodils dancing, is missing.

Wordsworth's belief in 'Tintern Abbey' that 'Nature never did betray/The heart that loved her' (ll.123–4) is reinforced in the early parts of ***The Prelude***. In this work, Wordsworth discovered a fresh approach to the epic theme of humankind and our environment. The poem in its entirety charts the development of the poet's creative imagination. Importantly, Books 1 and 2 tell how, during his formative years, Wordsworth received profound impressions of a moral power in nature. Nature, he wrote, 'Peopled my mind with beauteous forms or grand/And made me love them ... And, in our dawn of being, constitute/The bond of union betwixt life and joy' (Bk.1, ll.573–85). These lines evoke a boy's deeply felt sense of communion with his surroundings, experienced while walking in the woods. While the first-person speaker in *The Prelude* is Wordsworth, the poem is not strictly autobiographical.

The boy's sensual enjoyment of nature – 'It was a time of rapture' (Bk.1, l.457) – is evident in passages such as the one describing the pleasures of skating 'in the frosty season' (Bk.1, l.452). Here, Wordsworth's perceptions colour the world for us as we, by reading the poem, re-create the scene of his composition for ourselves. At sunset, when he should have been returning home, the boy 'wheeled about/Proud and exultant *like* an untired horse' (Bk.1, l.459). The simile here compares the boy's energetic steps to those of a galloping steed. The image is reinforced with 'All shod with steel' (Bk.1, l.460) – both the horse and the boy are wearing steel shoes – as the poem invokes the traditional country chase of the 'hunted hare' (Bk.1, l.464): the alliteration strengthens the liveliness of the picture of both horses and skaters racing along. The lines, 'The leafless trees and every icy crag/ Tinkled like iron' (Bk.1, ll.468–9) ingeniously continue the 'steel' image, as the boys give their 'bodies to the wind' (Bk.1, l.479) until 'The orange sky of evening died away' (Bk.1, l.473) and the spinning world stops 'short' (Bk.1, l.484). The wider implication is that the spinning skaters represent the frantic nature of human activity, which must cease if we are to understand our place in the world through contemplating nature.

In this extended image of boys skating, Wordsworth creates the same kind of subtle and flexible movement as in the 'daffodils' rhythm. The boys wheel and turn and the stars wheel with them; even after they stop, the sensation of the cliffs continuing to whirl is effectively rendered – 'I ... stopped short; yet the solitary cliffs/Wheeled by me'

(Bk.1, ll.483–5). But more is implied here, for the boys are subject to natural laws that are ultimately indifferent to them. The passage is successful because the images of the boys skating are both authentic and concrete. Wordsworth is less sure-footed in lines where he invokes vague images such as the abstract 'Ye Presences of Nature, in the sky/ Or on the earth ... Work like a sea?' (Bk.1, ll.490–501).

- The above passage is packed with images of movement. Note verbs such as 'wheeled', 'hissed', 'flew' and 'spinning'.
- Equally evocative are the adjectives and verbs that paint glittering images, such as 'blazed', 'tinkled', 'gleamed' (v); 'polished', 'sparkling', 'glassy' (adj).

Key point

It is also useful to compare these passages in *The Prelude* with those that render a description of Wordsworth's first experience of the Simplon Pass in the Alps (Book VI, ll.452–572) as a young adult. This poem features a more mature appreciation of nature and the awe it inspires in him; but it also points to the disappointment of the reality after he had imagined and anticipated an overwhelming grandeur. The final achievement of crossing the Alps, he thinks, ought to be more significant than it actually is.

In *The Prelude* Wordsworth demonstrates the forceful way he brings his experiences before the reader, drawing conclusions that seem like an integral part of the experience itself. This is a common characteristic of all his work. (Note that the version of *The Prelude* given in the *Selected Poems* ought to be compared with other versions, because there are many variations.)

Wordsworth's powerful imagination is shown at its best in **'Yew-Trees'** (p.172). Here his third-person speaker imagines, through an extended metaphor, that the one yew tree supplied the branches that were made into weapons used in the English victories in the late medieval wars against Scotland and France. The yew is an evergreen tree 'Produced too slowly ever to decay/Of form and aspect too magnificent/To be destroyed' (ll.11–13). The measured verse reflects the tree's magnificence and its eternal significance. From the solitary tree, the 'pride of Lorton Vale' (l.1), the speaker remembers an even more splendid stand, a 'fraternal Four of Borrowdale/Joined in one solemn and capacious grove' (ll.14–15). The alliteration here enhances the solemn tribute he pays to the trees. The intricate description of the 'Huge trunks! – and each particular trunk a growth/Of intertwisted fibres serpentine/Upcoiling, and inveterately convolved' (ll.16–18) captures the solidity of the yews and the power that emanates from them.

Through another extended metaphor, Wordsworth imagines the yews as timeless. In their shade – 'sable roof/Of boughs' (ll.23–4) – the great human emotions and concepts – 'Fear', 'trembling Hope', 'Silence and Foresight', 'Death' and 'Time the Shadow' (ll.26–8) – hold court on the 'altar' of this 'natural temple' (l.29).

Key point

This poem is a tour de force, illustrating the power of the imagination to imbue a mere tree with meaning beyond its outward form by using striking and memorable images. It could be of value to compare the use of the yew tree in this poem with those of other poets, such as Sylvia Plath, who used the yew tree as a powerful phallic symbol that dominates in a different way.

In his early years Wordsworth did not seek natural beauty simply for beauty's sake. Thus, it is a misreading of Wordsworth to conclude that he is a 'nature poet' because his perceptions of the role of nature go much deeper than a physical appreciation of nature. Rather, these early experiences induced in him a firm belief that 'Mankind and Nature' are, or ought to be, in partnership. This is evident in 'Yew-Trees', where an 'active principle' within the natural world coincides with certain basic needs of the human soul in a way that can produce harmony among the passions, hence bringing peace of mind. For Wordsworth, nature provides not just sensual pleasure, but also spiritual rejuvenation.

Images of man's work within nature

The imagery in several of Wordsworth's poems demonstrates that, despite his veneration of the natural world, he did not eschew (shun) man's work within nature. In the sonnet **'Composed Upon Westminster Bridge'** (pp.150–1), for example, the images show that cities, and their associated technologies, are an essential part of our existence and must be valued as such. Although he regretted the effects of the Industrial Revolution on ordinary people, Wordsworth did not condemn human encroachment on the environment. Such concerns about humanity's environmental impact had not yet surfaced in the collective consciousness in the early nineteenth century, when 'progress' was still something to be applauded. It was not until the mid–nineteenth century that Victorian poets such as Matthew Arnold rebelled against the encroachment of the Industrial Revolution's 'girdling city's hum', as Arnold depicts it in 'Lines Written in Kensington Gardens'. In this poem, Arnold describes seeking refuge in one of London's gardens from 'the huge world which roars hard by' (Arnold 1949, p.131).

In contrast, Wordsworth's images show London as 'A sight so touching in its majesty' (l.3) that, indeed, the entire planet 'has not anything to shew more fair:' (l.1). The insertion of the colon is important here because it indicates and accentuates the picture Wordsworth is about to create. The speaker's view of the city is qualified by distance: its 'Ships, towers, domes, theatres, and temples lie/Open unto the fields, and to the sky' (ll.6–7). Thus, Wordsworth is neither in the midst of Arnold's hellish 'city's jar' (Arnold, p.132) nor uncritically admiring man's edifices. Rather, he sees them clothed by 'The beauty of the morning' (l.5), an image that, as if in a painting, transforms man-made structures into objects of natural wonder. The similarity to a picture in poetry continues as the speaker sees even the 'mighty heart' of the city as 'lying still' (l.14).

The silence and stillness of Wordsworth's depiction of London is in stark contrast to what Arnold saw as 'men's impious uproar' (Arnold, p.132). The comparison of these two poems shows how Wordsworth, as a Romantic poet, shows little consciousness of the dangers of our aggressive assault on the natural environment, whereas the Victorian Arnold – half a century later – saw modernity as the epitome of man's destructiveness.

A closer reading of the poem shows the extent to which Wordsworth's imagination was captivated by the sight of London in the early morning light. As in so many of his poems, this moment was recollected later in tranquillity, for the sub-title of the poem misrepresents the facts. Wordsworth had passed over Westminster Bridge in July 1802, not September. He was, at the time, anxious and confused both by his divided political loyalties between France and England and by his feelings for Annette Vallon, whose child he was visiting for the first time. The moment he captures offers a brief respite from his personal turmoil. By resolving the issue of his allegiance to Vallon and the child, Wordsworth probably made a significant step in shedding the regrets of the past, a decision that marked a significant phase of change in his life.

As in many other poems by Wordsworth, the transforming effect of lived experience on the speaker is crucial to the structure of 'Composed Upon Westminster Bridge'. The claim that 'Dull would he be of soul who could pass by' (l.2) such a 'sight' (l.3), implies that the speaker and, by inference, his readers, are not among the dull of soul. Here, London has been so transformed by Wordsworth's imagination that he is able to negate the common view of the city as a noisy, filthy and squalid place. In Wordsworth's imagined London, even the air is 'smokeless' (l.8) and the city 'still'. The assertion that the city is 'majest[ic]', and the simile 'doth *like* a garment, wear/The beauty of the morning' (ll.4–5), create a compelling picture of the city wrapped in morning light. The adjectives 'bright and glittering' (l.8) evoke the sparkle of the sun's rays at sunrise. Looking at London through the speaker's eyes totally transforms the city – not only because its power is dormant, but also because he sees it as part of the 'splendor' of nature in its entirety as revealed in the sun's first light, at one with 'valley, rock, or hill' (l.10).

Significantly, the rhyme scheme changes at this point as the speaker suggests that the sun is shining on the first day of a new creation. The verb 'steep' (l.9), meaning to 'impregnate with', suggests that the power of the sun can transform an entire city. This is qualified with the adverb 'beautifully', reinforcing the beneficence of the sun's authority. At this rhyming change, the focus is directed to the effect of this altered view of the city on the speaker, for it brings him a 'calm so deep' (l.11). Importantly, the emphasis has shifted to the speaker's feelings rather than on what he is seeing. The emphatic 'Dear God!' (l.13) circles back to the reference to 'soul' in the second line, calling forth praise for the speaker's revelation, and consequently for the possibilities it offers for a spiritual revelation for humanity.

Similarly, in the sonnet **'Steamboats, Viaducts, and Railways'** (see the Appendix), Wordsworth shows an acceptance of the necessity of man's work in nature, for in their 'harsh features' (l.10), 'Nature doth embrace/ Her lawful offspring in Man's art' (ll.10–11). This much later poem suggests that even though human edifices are seen to 'mar/The loveliness of Nature' (ll.4–5), 'Time' is 'Pleased' with our 'triumphs o'er his brother Space' (ll.11–12). Wordsworth sees these works as offering 'hope' (l.14), showing he is not merely a poet of nature; he suggests that the natural world must accommodate human activity.

- Also consider the way in which St Paul's Cathedral is represented in 'St Paul's' (pp.170–1).

Key point

Through poems such as 'Steamboats, Viaducts, and Railways' and 'Composed Upon Westminster Bridge', Wordsworth shows that the transforming power of the imagination can re-order our existence so that humankind's creations are encompassed within the natural world rather than remaining distinct from it.

Images of rustics

Some of Wordsworth's most memorable poems centre on commonplace figures in the English countryside. Wordsworth uses these figures to illustrate the theories behind Romantic poetry more effectively: that nothing is too trivial to be the source of a poetic moment, that any ordinary event can be transformed through the power of the imagination. Because they are part of the natural world, these rustics, peasants, shepherds and ordinary folk – 'Whom I already loved … for the fields and hills/Where was their occupation and abode' ('Michael', ll.24–7, p.115) – have something to teach the poet and, by extension, his readers.

One such figure is the **'Solitary Reaper'** (pp.165–6) – a rare example of recording an experience that is not Wordsworth's own – who brings a sense of joy to the speaker and inspires him to abandon his melancholy mood. The first line, 'Behold her, single in the field', immediately strikes a chord in the reader/listener who is struck by her singularity, underlined by the emphatic opening word: 'Behold'. This is reinforced by the second line which emphasises her 'solitar[iness]'. In the first three lines, then, she is described as 'single', 'solitary' and 'by herself', as the speaker skilfully describes her striking presence in the field. Again, in line 5, she is 'Alone' while line 4 makes it clear that she is not to be, or will not be, disturbed in her work. Her status is further emphasised by the 'melancholy' (l.6) refrain she sings 'by herself' (l.3) that fills the valley with 'sound' (l.8) and reflects the speaker's own frame of mind.

The nature of the song she sings is characterised in the second stanza and it is this song, rather than the figure of the girl, that is central to the poem. The song is defined through comparisons with other songs and singers, a method of comparison that attempts to define the undefinable. The song is better than a Nightingale's (l.9), which is said to be the sweetest birdsong in the world and is 'sweet[er]' (l.10) than an uplifting tune heard out in the desert by weary 'Travellers' (l.11). Also, no Cuckoo ever had a 'sweeter voice', even though its song might be heard as far away as the Hebrides islands north of Britain (ll.13–16). The song, then, is more haunting and extraordinary than any other sound the speaker has heard, and it has an inspirational effect on him.

The poem is less concerned with describing the scene than with what the speaker is thinking. This becomes apparent in the third stanza when the speaker pleads to be told not just the song's message, but also the events that lie behind it. He speculates on the origin of the song, noting that it almost has the plaintive strains of a hymn. 'Perhaps' (l.18), he wonders, it is an echo of past battles, representing something 'unhappy' (l.19). Or, he suggests, it might just be a humble peasant refrain about personal 'sorrow, loss, or pain' (l.23), intoning the sense of loss that is always with us. (Interestingly, in the passage in Thomas Wilkinson's *Tour of Scotland* (1824) describing a highland girl singing while she reaps, which Wordsworth had seen in manuscript, she sings in Erse, the Gaelic language of Scotland.)

Whatever its nature, the song has a remarkable effect on the speaker. It does not matter what the reaper is singing, after all, because the sight of her 'singing at her work' (l.27) inspires in him a sense of joy. Moreover, the impression she makes allows him to capture the melody for himself through his imagination and feeling. He has 'listened till I had my fill' (l.29; in Wordsworth's later, revised versions of the poem this appears as the more effective 'listened, motionless and still'), but departs spiritually enlightened and elated, taking with him in his 'heart' (l.31) the unique music she has fashioned for him.

For this poem Wordsworth chooses a regular rhyme scheme that mirrors the resonance of the reaper's own song. The first four lines of each eight-line stanza have an alternating rhyme, and each stanza finishes with two rhyming couplets. This creates the effect of the sound echoing the sense of the scene. In the last stanza, the two-syllable end words – 'ending' and 'bending' – have the effect of extending the notes of the girl's song to make them seem even more mournful, and thus more memorable, for the speaker.

- The emphasis in this poem is on the faculty of hearing rather than seeing.
- The adjectives chosen are particularly evocative of a sad refrain, such as 'weary', 'shady' and 'plaintive'.
- For a poem with a remarkably similar attitude to thought processes, see Wallace Stevens's poem 'Idea of Order at Key West' (Stevens 1972).

In **'Resolution and Independence'** (pp.137–42) Wordsworth presents us with the ultimate rustic in the person of an old leech-gatherer, who confirms his belief that ordinary folk best demonstrate his theory of how the imagination can be used to bring humankind and nature into conjunction. Wordsworth's leech-gatherer is so close to nature that he seems himself to be a natural object; at the same time, though, he remains intensely human. This poem is a profound comment on human life and, more particularly, on the life of a poet.

The poet/speaker begins in a state of melancholy. He is walking alone on the moor and, despite the bright morning, is despondent. The first two stanzas are a vivid rendering of a natural scene, describing the intense clarity of the sky after a storm. Wordsworth, at his best, shows us the primal joy of existence, dominated by images of fertility such as the 'Stock-dove broods' (l.5) and 'morning's birth' (l.9). There is action everywhere as the 'Magpie chatters' (l.6) and 'The Hare is running' (l.11), while the earth is renewed with 'The grass is bright with rain-drops' (l.10). This background is conveyed in the third person, so that the start of the third stanza marks a sudden change. The omniscient narration gives way to that of first person as the speaker interposes his own presence: 'I was a Traveller then upon the moor' (l.15). From this point on, the poem chronicles the speaker's own experiences. Importantly, the subject is the speaker himself and not the leech-gatherer.

Human existence, 'so vain and melancholy' (l.21), is shown as dissonant in comparison with the harmonious existence of nature, as the speaker sketches his own personal crisis. The fourth stanza expresses his anxiety about the balancing of pain and joy – 'As high as we have mounted in delight/In our dejection do we sink as low' (ll.24–5) – implying that a poet feels these extremes more acutely than the general population. And as expressed in his earlier poem, 'Strange Fits of Passion Have I Known' (see below), the speaker is beset by irrational fears – 'fears and fancies thick upon me came/Dim sadness – and blind thoughts' (ll.27–8). He elaborates on these thoughts, even supposing that perhaps to be a poet means being condemned to misery and defeat like the talented poet

Chatterton (l.43) who, in loneliness and poverty, poisoned himself at the age of seventeen. (In so doing he became a symbol for the Romantics of a neglected young genius.) Thus, from stanzas three to seven, the poet speculates that the pleasures of the 'happy Child of earth' (l.31) he enjoys might not last: 'another day' (l.34) might bring 'Solitude, pain of heart, distress, and poverty' (l.35). This morbid introspection becomes the subject of the poem until the eighth stanza.

After elaborating upon such depressing thoughts, in stanza eight the outside world breaks in again in the shape of the leech-gatherer: 'I saw a Man before me unawares' (l.55). The sudden appearance of the old man immediately suggests a prophetic presence, for he is in a 'lonely place' (l.52) and the 'oldest Man he seemed that ever wore gray hairs' (l.56). He also appears to be a natural object, as Wordsworth employs an extended simile: '*As* a huge stone … there to sun itself' (l.64–70).

This is a striking image, enhanced by the internal simile '*Like* a Sea-beast crawled forth' (l.69), because it makes the man appear to be part of a primeval age rather than merely human. In a shift away from the restlessness of the preceding stanzas, here the description moves forward with deliberation, creating a sense of primitive strength and reliability in contrast to the confusion of the speaker's thoughts. The image is reinforced in stanza ten where 'this Man' is 'not all alive nor dead/Nor all asleep' (ll.71–2), and yet we wonder at the man's powers of resistance, for he is the bearer of pain and suffering. A further simile: 'Motionless *as* a Cloud' (l.82) strengthens the rock-like image and extends the air of mystery previously established.

Up to this point the old man has only been seen at the fringes of the poet's consciousness. However, from the eleventh stanza the poem traces the gradual penetration of the old man's significance into the speaker's mind: he has the strength of mind, dignity and composure that the poet, in his present state, cannot claim to have. When the leech-gatherer is addressed, 'surprize' (l.97) breaks from 'a fire about his eyes' (l.97; in later versions this appears as the more effective: 'the sable orbs of his yet-vivid eyes'), suggesting a spiritual intensity. These images, together with 'his long gray Staff' (l.79), the way he cons (examines) the 'muddy water' (l.87), the simile '*As* if he had been reading in a book' (l.88) and his being 'above the reach/Of ordinary men' (ll.102–3), all support the idea of the man as a seer or prophet; this is, indeed, what he becomes for the speaker.

Importantly, his discovery of the leeches in stanza fifteen, his 'Employment hazardous and wearisome' (l.108), the 'many hardships' he has to 'endure' (l.109) and his roaming 'From Pond to Pond ... from moor to moor' (l.110) parallels the writing of poems. The similes '*Like* one whom I had met with in a dream' (l.117) and '*like* a Man from some far region sent' (l.118) emphasise the speaker's interpretation of the man as a spiritual messenger. Stanzas eighteen and nineteen are central to the poem, because the meditation on human mortality spells out our ultimate fate:

> the fear that kills;
> The hope that is unwilling to be fed;
> Cold, pain, and labour, and all fleshly ills;
> And mighty Poets in their misery dead. (ll.120–3)

The leech-gatherer's answer addresses the difficulty of maintaining human fortitude, resolution and independence in the face of adversity, because he explains that increased knowledge can only be won at the expense of increased pain. Stanza twenty shows, moreover, that this endless search must be continued. The whole force of the poet's realisation is compressed into the lines: 'I seemed to see him pace/About the weary moors continually/Wandering about alone and silently' (ll.136–8).

The long, dragging syllables in these lines dramatically slows the poem's pace. The end of the word 'continually' is reached with great effort, only for the same wearying pace to continue relentlessly into the next line. This stagnant rhythm imitates the old man's unremitting, patient, plodding pace. From observing the old man, the speaker learns that 'persevere[nce]' (l.133) and persistence are the keys to creating and maintaining human commitment.

Key point

In this poem of affirmation and moral force, the poet elevates the leech-gatherer into a mythic figure who speaks profound truths about universal human endeavour. 'Resolution and Independence' is a key poem in Wordsworth's oeuvre because it clearly shows the basic application of his method. Firstly, the freshness of the natural world is described in the third person; this relatively detached perspective gives way to the speaker/poet's first-person emotional involvement with the old man. And secondly, after the speaker describes his depressed mood, the poem's affirmative resolution shows how he resolves those feelings of melancholy and hopelessness through the spiritual enlightenment provided by the leech-gatherer's profound knowledge of his place in the universe.

NARRATIVE VOICE

Personae or speakers

Most of Wordsworth's poems tell a story through a speaker or narrator, usually called a 'persona'. It is important to work out the story of the poem, and its central thought or mood, before beginning an analysis of its features. Establishing the identity of the poem's persona, or speaker, is also essential in making sense of the poem's central message.

Wordsworth often casts himself in the speaker's role, although we must be careful not to confuse the poet with the historical person. In acting as a narrator for his poems, Wordsworth claims to speak universally. Acting as the first-person speaker in his poems, Wordsworth is able to recount his first-hand experiences directly to readers, a technique that enables him to involve his readers directly in the experience. Occasionally, he chooses the third-person omniscient narrative voice, which is used to describe the action and the characters from a more removed, objective perspective.

The persona is also used to establish the voice and tone of the poem. Wordsworth's deployment of a first-person speaker/narrator allows him to convey the immediacy of his experiences and engage his readers. In some poems, however, the narrative strategy is more complex, particularly in the longer poems.

Complex narration

In the long narrative poems 'Resolution and Independence' and 'The Ruined Cottage', both the story (or at least part of it) and Wordsworth's philosophy are conveyed through a character within the poem who is described in the third person (as 'he', 'the old man' etc.) by the poet/speaker. This character serves not only to tell a tale but also to offer the poet/speaker, as well as the poem's readers, some key insights into the human condition.

In **'The Ruined Cottage'** (pp.3–18), the speaker comes across a 'wanderer' or 'old man' who tells him that the derelict garden they stumble upon is intimately connected to a woman's sad 'tale of silent suffering' (l.233). In telling his story, the wanderer effectively becomes the narrator. His storytelling ability is immediately apparent to the poet/speaker, who admiringly notes that the man 'had rehearsed/[Margaret's] homely tale with such familiar power ... that the things of which he spake/Seemed present' (ll.208–12), an ability that deeply moves the speaker.

The poet/speaker, then, conveys to the reader both his own reactions to Margaret's story and the wanderer/narrator's reactions. A third level of narration is created when Margaret herself begins to tell her story. Although there are, in fact, three speakers, the poem seamlessly weaves their stories together into an intricate and complex narrative.

Although the fact of Margaret's death is established early in the poem, Margaret's story of loss and desertion gains momentum throughout. The wanderer/narrator charts Margaret's slide towards death through his various visits over a period of time. As this slow descent is clearly marked by the seasons, both the poet/speaker and the poem's readers are able to understand and empathise with her bitter decline. Margaret's experiences turn this formerly cheerful wife and mother into a destroyed woman, weighed down first by the desertion of her husband and then by the subsequent loss of her children, a tragedy commemorated with 'the corner-stones/Till then unmarked, on either side the door' (ll.330–1). The wanderer/narrator's story is interspersed with comments addressed directly to the poet/speaker, such as 'It would have grieved/Your very heart to see her. Sir, I feel/The story linger in my heart' (ll.361–4), interjections that remind the reader of the continuing conversation taking place between them.

Margaret's goodness is at the centre of the poem. Even her grief and despair, which are eventually 'caught' by 'Her infant babe' (l.409–10) who subsequently dies, cannot efface her fundamental decency and kindness. The progress of decay in a garden once bright with flowers mirrors the woman's decline towards death from 'sorrow' (l.431).

Like the leech-gatherer in 'Resolution and Independence', the wanderer/narrator assumes the guise of a man of deep wisdom who, as well as telling Margaret's story, is employed to make the point that we must learn from sorrow instead of being bowed down by it. His thoughts are interposed at regular intervals throughout his discourse (ll.67–88; ll.188–98; ll.221–36; ll.363–75; ll.508–25), allowing Wordsworth to express the poem's central idea that 'there is often found/In mournful thoughts ... A power to virtue' (ll.227–9). Without this sense of virtue through suffering, the wanderer/narrator recognises that he would be seen only as 'An idle dreamer' (l.231). He reiterates these thoughts at the end of the poem when he tells the poet/speaker to 'Be wise and chearful' (l.510) for 'She sleeps in the calm earth, and peace is here' (l.512). The poet/speaker must learn from the example he is shown that emotional repose is only possible through spiritual forbearance.

The wanderer/narrator is also used to comment on the poet's purpose. It is the poets who must tell Margaret's tale and others like it, for it is their trade to 'call upon the hill and streams to mourn ... for they speak ... with a voice/Obedient to the strong creative power/Of human passion' (ll.75–9). Wordsworth goes further to tell us that poets must call upon our 'Sympathies' (l.79) because they 'steal upon the meditative mind/And grow with thought' (ll.81–2). Clearly, this imperative is consistent with his core belief that through the power of thought and the creative imagination we can dispel our sorrow, bring joy and understand our human passions.

When the 'old Man' (l.493) ceases his story, he sees that the poet/speaker is 'moved' (l.493). Indeed, his listener is so affected that he 'turned aside in weakness, nor had power/To thank him for the tale' (ll.495–6). What he gains from it is the wisdom that the 'secret spirit of humanity ... still survived' (ll.503–6). The wanderer/narrator acts as a seer who conveys the wisdom:

That what we feel of sorrow and despair
From ruin and from change, and all the grief
The passing shews of being leave behind,
Appeared an idle dream that could not live
Where meditation was. (ll.520–4)

The tale's central message – to be 'wise and chearful' (l.510), and to find beauty amidst despair through the power of the creative imagination – is conveyed to the poet/speaker through the story of Margaret told by the wanderer/narrator. This seemingly convoluted narrative strategy is a successful method, in this poem at least, of presenting Wordsworth's philosophy that human values can only be understood through extended contemplation.

A similar narration strategy is adopted for **'Resolution and Independence'** (pp.137–42; see also above under 'Images of rustics'), in which the poet/speaker encounters a travelling leech-gatherer who lifts him out of his 'dejection' (l.25) and teaches him that perseverance can overcome despair. The narration strategy here, though, is less complex than in 'The Ruined Cottage': most of the story is told by the poet/speaker and the leech-gatherer has only a few lines of direct speech (ll.131–3). Most of what 'he told' (l.106), and his 'stately speech' (l.103), is merely described. The emphasis is placed on the leech-gatherer's effect on the poet/speaker, rather than on the gatherer's character traits.

Third-person narration

A much simpler narration strategy is adopted in another long narrative poem, **'Michael'** (pp.114–27). Unlike 'Resolution and Independence' and 'The Ruined Cottage', both of which are narrated in the first person, Michael's story is told in the third person; it is about him, but is not told by him. Michael's character, however, is often revealed through direct speech, particularly in his conversations with his son Luke. This represents a more conventional narrative technique than Wordsworth uses in his other long poems, but its simplicity does not make it less effective.

In a brief introduction, the speaker does use the first-person 'I' to explain that he is relating the story because he has been deeply moved by Michael's insights into 'the heart of man and human life' (l.33). However, once Michael's story actually begins (l.40), the speaker adopts a more remote perspective and is not himself a participant in the story. The poem concludes with the end of Michael's story rather than returning to discuss what the speaker has learned from it, as in 'The Ruined Cottage' and the brief ending of 'Resolution and Independence'.

First-person narration

On the other hand, the Odes, like most of Wordsworth's poems, utilise a first-person speaker. **'Ode: Intimations of Immortality'** (pp.157–63), for example, is a meditative poem that celebrates the poet's view of our place in the universe. He laments that when he was young he saw the truth of nature when 'The earth, and every common sight/To me did seem/Apparelled in celestial light/The glory and the freshness of a dream' (ll.2–5). Now, even though 'The Rainbow comes and goes/And lovely is the Rose' (ll.10–11), he is no longer able to sense that glory. Instead, he sets humankind within the wider pattern of nature portrayed in stanza three, as he develops the theme that successfully reaching maturity forces us to leave behind the freshness and joy of childhood, meaning that we can no longer enjoy life with the same level of spontaneity.

Wordsworth develops the poem through the different stages of a person's growth, equating these stages with actors' roles. In stanza seven the speaker declares that our human fate requires us to play one role after another throughout our lives. Stanza eight praises the child as the 'best Philosopher' (l.110), but notes that the child cannot preserve, and cannot realise, what is open to them. Wordsworth's speaker ironically underlines the paradox that the child is the bearer of a heavenly message of joy while also being the eager agent of their own imprisonment in the world of the senses, a contradiction expressed in the lines, 'Full soon thy Soul shall have her earthly freight/And custom lie upon thee with a weight/

Heavy as frost' (ll.129–30; note the simile here). Yet, the speaker argues that the 'Delight and liberty' (l.139) of childhood sustains us in the world of darkness, for 'Those shadowy recollections ... Are yet the fountain light of all our day' (ll.152–4).

The speaker in this poem is intent on showing us that making an imaginative return to the spontaneity of childhood is possible in adulthood. Both he and his audience receive the religious affirmation that humans are intrinsically a part of the totality of the universe. We must, therefore, come to terms with our own existence and achieve a tranquil state of contemplation, rather than grieve over our losses. Through thought and reflection we, like the speaker, can reach the point where we can still achieve a state of spiritual innocence without succumbing to religious doctrines. The speaker's understanding that participation in life's joys is possible through contemplation is intended to provide readers with a renewed confidence in life's intrinsic value.

A simple version of the philosophy that underpins 'Ode: Intimations of immortality' can be found in the early poem **'Lines Written in Early Spring'** (pp.53–4). Clearly expressing the speaker's recollections of nature and an accompanying state of tranquillity, the poem is a straightforward summation of Wordsworth's main ideas about nature and the centrality of the imagination. The opening of the poem demonstrates this idea, as the 'I' speaker 'heard a thousand blended notes/While in a grove I sate reclined' (ll.1–2). Nature, as in the unspoiled landscapes he so loves, is 'link[ed]' irrevocably to 'The human soul' (ll.5–6), and he laments how 'grieved' his heart is 'to think/What man has made of man' (ll.7–8). All around him the birds 'hopped and played' (l.13), bringing him 'a thrill of pleasure' (l.16), and the speaker realises that he 'must think' (l.19) to remember the past pleasures that nature provided him with. Echoing the 'Ode', the speaker's 'sad thoughts' (l.4) can be dispelled only by the realisation that a contemplation of nature brings understanding.

Later, in the 'Ode: Intimations of Immortality', Wordsworth provides a more complete answer to the question of 'what man has made of man' when his speaker finally understands that life's value can be comprehended by recognising our place within the universe. The device of the first-person speaker is used more directly in 'Lines Written in Early Spring' than in the 'Ode'; in both poems, Wordsworth effectively uses this narrative technique to present his main ideas about life and the poetic imagination, although this is achieved more successfully in the later poem.

Key point

The importance of Wordsworth's narrative strategy to the success of his poetry cannot be overstated. Although he varies the narrative voice, it is usually with the use of the device of the first-person speaker that he achieves the greatest facility. This tool allows him not only to represent the speaker's character, but also to present his main ideas about the achievement of a spiritual reconciliation between man and the universe through contemplation.

THEMES, IDEAS & VALUES

The wisdom of childhood

Children, in Wordsworth's poems, are presented as individuals, and are often idealised as sources of superior wisdom to adults. Before the Romantics, the child was viewed as a small adult, contaminated by original sin, who had to be disciplined by adults to attain a state of grace. Because it was believed that the capacity for reason came some time after puberty, adults would act and reason on children's behalf.

Yet, for Wordsworth in particular, the child came to represent spontaneity rather than depravity and incompleteness. He saw the child as possessing a kind of essential wisdom, allowing it access to truths that were barred to adults. As well as being free from sin, the child was privileged with great insight into the human condition, a gift that was lost in adulthood.

Childhood and spiritual understanding

In his own childhood Wordsworth became absorbed in the natural beauty he saw around him, conscious of the variations brought about by the weather and the change in seasons. He became an observer of the children he knew most intimately, noting their engrossment in activities and games that seemed remote from adult consciousness. Because he lacked the knowledge to explain the basis for children's seemingly unfettered happiness in scientific or psychological terms, he adopted a theory of 'pre-existence', whereby a child has a deep spiritual knowledge at birth that gradually decays in maturity and can only be recalled through meditative recollection.

In **'We Are Seven'** (pp.56–9), for example, the 'little cottage Girl' (l.5) with 'a rustic, woodland air' (l.9) demonstrates a greater insight than her adult interrogator. Her dead brother and sister remain, for her, part of the family and are included in her daily activities as if they are alive. The child refuses to accept the interrogator's assertion that 'they are dead; those two are dead' (l.65), claiming instead that 'Their graves are green, they may be seen' (l.37). Clearly, death does not hold the same significance for her as it does for adults, and this alternative viewpoint makes the adult interrogator feel uncomfortable.

Key point

Wordsworth suggests that the innocence of children shows us a fresh truth, a new way of seeing. Even in this early poem, the path that Wordsworth's later poetry will address is mapped out.

In 'We Are Seven', the stanzas of question and answer alternate in a rhythmic pattern of four-beat followed by three-beat lines, an alternation that highlights both the insistence of the interrogator and the confidence and certainty of the child. We are told in the first line that she is 'A simple Child', and this simplicity is reflected in the effortlessness with which she delivers her straightforward answers, which are nonetheless insightful. She is one of Wordsworth's rustics (see 'Images of rustics' above), who illustrates Wordsworth's belief that simple folk can manifest a clearer judgment.

Similarly, in the short poem **'My heart leaps up'** (p.135) Wordsworth argues, paradoxically, that 'The Child is Father of the Man' (l.7), indicating that the character and interests of the adult are determined by the influences upon, and the developed sentiments of, early youth. Exploring the child's instinctive impulse to discover truths about the natural world, he also notes the loss of this basic impulse in adulthood. We learn the gift for such pleasure in childhood – 'So was it when my life began' (l.3) – and Wordsworth urges us to carry this primal response forward, through adolescence into adulthood, pleading 'So be it when I shall grow old/ Or let me die' (ll.5–6). This poem celebrates the child's view of life while expressing fears that the child's view of nature's majesty may be dimmed during adulthood. However, it also conveys the hope that nature will continue to move the narrator as an adult, as it did in childhood.

In Wordsworth's poetry, the figure of the child is elevated to near-sacred status. Children are destined for 'heaven' ('Abraham's bosom') as Wordsworth explains in the sonnet **'It is a beauteous Evening'** (p.149). While walking with his daughter, Caroline, in France for the first time, he sees the natural world reflecting this special moment. The evening is 'calm and free' (l.1); it is a 'holy time' (l.2), 'Breathless with adoration' (l.3), and this bountiful love includes his daughter. The 'mighty Being' (l.6) (the Spirit of Nature) is 'eternal' (l.7) and 'everlastingly' (l.8) available as a source of creative inspiration. The child is untouched by the adult speaker's own 'solemn thought' (l.10), not yet knowing the cares of the world; 'divine' (l.11), because unaffected by worry; and in possession of an ability to see nature afresh that is denied to adults.

Recollecting childhood insights

In stanza five of **'Ode: Intimations of Immortality'** (pp.157–63), Wordsworth struggles to explain why children are happy in their independence, reaching the conclusion that we come into the world from a pre-existent state of greater perfection and happiness: 'Our birth is but a sleep and a forgetting' (l.58) and we are born 'Not in entire forgetfulness/And not in utter nakedness/But trailing clouds of glory … From God' (ll.62–5).

Later, children's natural happiness, their 'vision splendid' (l.73), 'die[s] away' (l.75) and can only be experienced in recollection. 'Heaven lies about us in our infancy' (l.66), but as we grow up 'Shades of the prison-house begin to close' (l.67), causing everything to become commonplace. The 'Youth, who daily farther from the East/Must travel' (ll.72–5), is closely bonded to nature while he grows. The child, Wordsworth believes, is the natural 'best Philosopher' (l.110). From this point in the poem, Wordsworth charts the course of the adult's descent into arid maturity, a state from which he can only be rescued through thought and contemplation.

Yet the ending of the poem qualifies this earlier belief, for the last stanza shows that the adult speaker is able to come to terms with his mature existence – 'The innocent brightness of a new-born Day/Is lovely yet' (ll.197–8). He takes comfort in his tranquil state of contemplation, rather than grieving at his loss of innocence. The adult is, after all, he concludes, a better philosopher than the child.

Wordsworth's interest in childhood was primarily due to his ability to use recollection to relive the imaginative splendour of his youth. He extended this idea to the belief that children's imaginations endowed them with special creative powers.

- Refer also to *The Prelude* for further examples of Wordsworth's view of the importance of children and childhood in the creative process.

Family and community

The Industrial Revolution led to widespread feelings of rootlessness, as it cut many workers off from their homes, their family environments and the accompanying traditions. Wordsworth continually stresses the importance of family and community. In **'Michael'** (pp.114–27), for example, the simple shepherd guards his sheep while his wife, Isabel, 'Whose heart was in her house' (l.84), spins wool and flax – the very home-based industries that were overtaken by mechanisation. Disaster only strikes this idyllic rural existence when their only child, Luke, is forced to leave home because Michael is 'summoned to discharge [an old] forfeiture' (l.225) that amounts to 'half his substance' (l.227). After the close family unit is fractured, Luke, rather than 'repair[ing] this loss' (l.262) and keeping ownership of 'these fields of ours' (l.240), falls into 'ignominy and shame' (l.454). He is eventually compelled to 'hide' overseas while Michael dies with a broken heart.

This is one of Wordsworth's great narrative poems, memorable for the way in which the characters, particularly Michael himself, are fused with their natural surroundings, and for Wordsworth's complete control of the emotional implications of their history. The sense of community that existed earlier is no longer available to this couple in their time of dire need, although Isabel thinks back to a time when a collection was taken up for another 'parish boy – at the church door/They made a gathering for him, shillings, pence/And halfpennies' (ll.269–71) – and 'the Neighbours bought/A Basket, which they filled with Pedlar's wares' (ll.271–2). Isabel's 'face brightened' (l.283) when she remembered how the boy had become rich as a result of this community support, but her relief is momentary. She pleads with Luke not to leave them as they 'have no other Child but thee to lose/None to remember' (ll.306–7) but, inevitably, he must go. She resumes her work, 'And all the ensuing week the house appeared/As cheerful as a grove in spring' (ll.315–6; note the simile here).

The old shepherd is drawn as a man with all the strength and reliability of a tree or rock – 'stout of heart, and strong of limb' (l.42) as he roams 'the heights' alone (l.60) through 'many thousand mists' (l.59). The next line – 'That came to him, and left him, on the heights' (l.60) – effectively describes the drifting to and fro of a mist, while the old man stands as solid and fixed as a tree root. This passage clearly shows his natural affinity with the hills and fields in which he lives and works.

Wordsworth gains an emotional distance from his subject here that he does not always manage in some other poems, as he outlines the drama that afflicts this rustic shepherd. Patience and tenderness are the key qualities of the old man's character – 'with patient mind enforced/To acts of tenderness' (ll.166–7) – qualities that become especially apparent with the birth of his son late in his life. When Michael hears that he may be forced to sell some of his fields, preventing him from passing them on to his son, all the life is drained out of the verse as it is drained out of the old man: 'This un-looked for claim/At the first hearing, for a moment took/More hope out of his life than he supposed/That any old man ever could have lost' (ll.227–30). This is a statement of exhaustion and his individuality seems overshadowed – 'any old man' (l.230) – by his loss of hope.

The bitter disappointment surrounding his son causes the old man's strength to vanish, as is evident from the cessation of his work on the sheepfold he started to build with Luke, for 'many and many a day he thither went/And never lifted up a single stone' (ll.474–5). The family unit of which he was so proud disintegrates with news of his beloved Luke's disgrace and flight. The futility of his efforts is suggested by the repetition of the words 'many and many'; these last lines of this penultimate stanza are a symbolic representation of Michael's downtrodden state of mind.

As Michael accepts his part in the natural world, the strength of his body and mind, as well as his love of and grief for Luke, are all expressed in highly naturalistic terms. Finally, the fold he builds is intended to be a bridge between nature and man, but it remains incomplete, a monument to disappointment and despair. Isabel dies shortly after Michael and the 'estate/Was sold' (ll.483–4) to a stranger. With the breaking up of the family unit the last sense of community is also lost.

Wordsworth first heard this story while at Hawkshead and was deeply impressed by it. The narrative is plain without any attempt at embroidery, and the blank verse rhythmic pattern is well sustained. The climax of the story is told unpretentiously and the simple diction is supported by strong implicit emotion. Wordsworth invites the reader to understand and share the feelings of an old shepherd whose struggle to keep his property in the hands of his own family is defeated by the imprudence and disgrace of his only son. That this should happen when the son has been loved and adored by his parents is incomprehensible to Michael, and emotionally affecting for the poem's readers.

Key point

This poem best illustrates that Wordsworth's beliefs in the inalienable rights and dignity of humankind did not change over the course of his career.

Q Which other poems show Wordsworth's respect for family and community?

Loss

Loss, and the despair it brings, is implicit in many of Wordsworth's poems. **'Lucy Gray'** (pp.73–5), for example, depicts the pathos caused by the loss of a child. When Lucy's father sends her out on a dark afternoon to light the way home for her mother, she is caught in a storm, becomes lost, and is swept from a bridge to her death.

As is customary in Wordsworth's poetry, the story is established through a persona who hears of the parents' loss. The first three stanzas present the background facts – that Lucy Gray is 'solitary' (l.4) and dwells on a lonely 'Moor' (l.6) – heightening the drama and preparing readers for what follows. The speaker remarks upon the absence of 'The sweetest Thing that ever grew' (l.7) as a way of establishing the narrative.

It is from stanza eight that the real tragedy occurs. The opening line, 'The storm came on before its time' (l.29), warns us that Lucy Gray is in danger. From the point where she 'never reached the Town' (l.32), we know that she is lost – a fact that is confirmed when 'The wretched Parents all that night/Went shouting far and wide' (ll.33–4), a statement that realistically re-creates their anguish.

Wordsworth crafts an authentic sense of distress as 'the Mother spied/ The print of Lucy's feet' (ll.43–4). For a moment there is hope that she will be found, as 'They tracked the footmarks small' (l.46) from 'the steep hill' (l.45) through a 'hedge' (l.47) and by a 'wall' (l.48) to 'an open field' (l.49), and we go with them, hoping, like them, that she will be found alive. The footmarks disappear 'Into the middle of the plank' (l.55) of the bridge, and no others are found. The distress of the parents is not dwelt upon at length, but is nevertheless vivid.

The speculation that Lucy is a wraith who wanders 'the lonesome Wild' (l.60) in the final two stanzas adds little to the narrative, but the poem conveys the profound sense of loss caused by the death of a child, demonstrating Wordsworth's sympathy for human pain and suffering.

Key point

This poem can be compared with **'Three years she grew'** (pp.77–8), in which the poet creates the persona of a child – also called Lucy – who grows to mature beauty in six stanzas, and then produces a dramatic reversal of expectations in the seventh. After her death, Lucy is only a memory. Wordsworth is demonstrating a universal truth about human existence: that life and death are, inevitably, creative opposites.

The long narrative poem **'The Ruined Cottage'** (pp.3–18) is the story of a father's callous abandonment of his wife and children. The order of Margaret's life gradually fragments after her husband's desertion, a decline reflected in her previously well-tended garden. Now 'weeds defaced' (l.415) the hardened soil; there is 'black mould' (l.416) and 'No winter greenness' (l.417).

The poem's tale is related through a series of flashbacks. It is established early that Margaret 'is dead' (l.103) as the speaker comes upon a wanderer (l.46), a prophet-like figure who reveals deep truths about life and death. Claiming that 'I see around me here/Things which you cannot see' (ll.67–8), the wanderer then relates what appears to be Wordsworth's essential philosophy about the nature of life and death:

> We die, my Friend,
> Nor we alone, but that which each man loved
> And prized in his peculiar nook of earth
> Dies with him. (ll.68–71)

Margaret's garden has died as a reflection of her pain and suffering. She had always given the wanderer 'A daughter's welcome' (l.95) but, he tells the speaker, 'the good die first' (l.96). Margaret herself connects the decline of her world of ordered nature with the source of her sorrow, fearing that the tree 'will be dead and gone/Ere Robert come again' (ll.425–6). Her sadness is not despair because she still hopes that her husband will return. Alas, 'she died/Last human tenant of these ruined walls' (ll.491–2).

Key point

The pathos of this scene clearly reflects Wordsworth's sensitivity to the sufferings of others. But he also makes clear that Margaret is not 'forgotten' as she fears. She is remembered by the old man, who tells the story that allows the speaker to immortalise her in the poem.

This poem poignantly brings Wordsworth's theme of human suffering and sorrow into a relationship of imaginative unity with the world of inanimate nature. Although the sense of loss here is overwhelming as the images of decay build up, Wordsworth qualifies that sense of loss by implying that the absence of the woman is compensated for by the fertility of nature.

- Like the old shepherd in 'Michael', the character of Margaret in 'The Ruined Cottage' is rendered with respect and sympathy for her anguish and gradual descent into grief.
- The sonnet 'Surprized by joy' (p.171) records the poet's personal anguish and sense of loss for his daughter, Catherine, who died in early childhood. Its poignancy stems from the absence of his loved one when he turns to share a special moment. 'Wind', as used in this poem, often refers symbolically to inspiration.
- Many of Wordsworth's poems deal with personal loss – see 'She dwelt among th' untrodden ways' (p.71) and 'The Thorn' (pp.30–7) as further examples.

Irrational fear and death

Although a slight poem, in **'Strange Fits of Passion Have I Known'** (see the Appendix for a later, revised version of this poem, which the following discussion refers to) Wordsworth still has a valid and powerful experience to communicate. This is done in the form of a lyrical ballad which tells the story of a lover who fears, irrationally, that his love might be dead.

The story is told briefly, using dramatic changes of emotion. The speaker/lover has felt 'Strange fits of passion' (l.1), a term referring to the tendency of lovers to think foolish thoughts on the slightest provocation. He is complacent, at first, as he goes to meet his girlfriend who looks 'like a rose in June' (l.6). This second stanza introduces an image of 'the moon' (l.9), which is about to set. As he moves on horseback at a 'quickening pace' (l.11) he climbs a 'hill' (l.14) and the image of the moon changes. It is now 'sinking' (l.15), coming 'near, nearer still' (l.16) in what seems to be a threatening manner. We know that this is irrational because the moon only rises and falls in relation to the earth's movement, but the lover is distracted by his thoughts and now the moon is 'descending' (l.20), appearing to come even closer by stanza six.

As his 'horse moved on; hoof after hoof' (l.21), the rhythm of the horse's hooves mimics clock time in contrast to the slow descent of the moon which has now 'dropped' (l.24). Of course, these four images of the moon are only an illusion, but the moon's apparent movement makes the speaker conscious of the limits imposed by mortality. The obscuring of the moon brings irrational fear into the lover's mind – 'What fond and wayward thoughts will slide/Into a lover's head!' (ll.25–6). He speculates, for no other reason than his awareness of the moon's downward path, that Lucy might 'be dead' (l.28).

Wordsworth captures exactly the kind of foolish thought that we sometimes have about our loved ones, suddenly imagining them overcome by disaster. In Wordsworth's original conception of the poem, he intended for the lover's fear to be justified at a later point; however, the poem is stronger for its ending on this note of delusional hysteria.

- Notice that the rhythm of the ballad echoes that of the horse's steps and that it quickens with the 'quickening pace' of the horse.
- Wordsworth was able to take a simple image, such as that of the moon's path, and create an effective poem around it.

In another short poem of great emotional force, **'A slumber did my spirit seal'** (p.71), Wordsworth exploits the contrast between the figurative language of the first stanza and the statement of cold fact in the second. In the first stanza the speaker is almost trance-like in his assurance that he has no 'human fears' (l.2) about an unnamed girl who is rendered as a somewhat trite figure, merely 'a thing that could not feel/The touch of early years' (ll.3–4). This stanza creates a sense of security and reassurance by its quiet, almost hypnotic, movement.

While the second stanza proceeds in the same gentle, even tone, it indicates the total destruction of the dream world created by the first. Now the girl, who is vaguely portrayed in the first, becomes authenticated by the literal fact of death, which puts her firmly beyond the reach of time.

The calmness of the stanza evokes the stillness of death, yet the tone of the poem is not one of resentment or desolation. Rather, it expresses a sort of desperate solace taken in the sense of peace and unity with nature that the girl achieves in death. Death for Wordsworth, then, represents a continuance of the cycle of life.

In ***The Prelude*** Book 1 (pp.188–204), the epic poem based on significant moments in Wordsworth's life, various themes are explored. The poet/speaker expresses an irrational fear when he recalls how he took a boat out without permission one summer evening. He set a course by a 'craggy ridge' (l.398) and rowed towards it. He 'dipped [his] oars into the silent Lake' and his boat 'Went heaving through the water, *like* a Swan' (ll.402–4; note the simile) when, unexpectedly, 'a huge Cliff … Upreared its head' (ll.406–8). The contrast between images here is striking. The peak's vague menace is established by the repetition of 'huge' (l.409) and the image of the cliff as a giant beast rearing up, aroused and threatening. The boy's panic is evident in the changed movement – 'I struck, and struck again' (l.408) – and the inexorable beat of the metre reflects the menace felt by the speaker as the passage moves steadily and relentlessly towards the awful climax: 'And growing still in stature, the huge Cliff/ Rose up between me and the stars' (ll.409–10). The sequence of events culminates in the narrator's paranoid belief that the shape 'like a living thing/Strode after me' (ll.411–12). This is an irrational fear, for the images seem to reflect the boy's feelings of guilt over his clandestine use of the boat, and he projects this guilt onto the landscape. This episode plunges the speaker into a dark mood that erases all the pleasant images of his surroundings from his mind.

The boy is subdued by his experience, but this is not merely a moral tale of a naughty boy being frightened by a mountain. Fear, even irrational fear, becomes capable of inspiring dignity and awe and, by sharing the poet's experiences, we are able to apprehend the sense of growth he is describing. Fear, according to Wordsworth, is only one strand of a child's complex emotional development.

Q In which other poems are there examples of irrational fear and death?

DIFFERENT INTERPRETATIONS

Different interpretations arise from different responses to a text. Over time, a text will evoke a wide range of responses from its readers, who may come from various social or cultural groups and live in very different places and historical periods. These responses can be published by critics and reviewers in newspapers, journals and books, or they can be expressed in discussions among readers in the media, classrooms, book groups and so on. While there is no single correct reading or interpretation of a text, it is important to understand that an interpretation is more than an 'opinion' – it is the justification of a point of view on the text. To present an interpretation of the text based on your point of view you must use a logical argument and support it with relevant evidence from the text.

Critical viewpoints

The first major body of Wordsworth criticism was produced by his contemporaries. This was mainly centred on the vast amount of his poetic oeuvre that did not reach the heights of his best poetry. It was commonly felt that Wordsworth, like many artists, did his best work in a relatively short period. For Wordsworth, this was the decade beginning around 1797 and ending around 1806, when he was still a young man. It is generally agreed that his poetic powers went into serious decline thereafter. The following excerpts are characteristic of the general commentary.

Byron, speaking about Wordsworth's long epic *The Excursion*, declaimed:

> Tis poetry – at least by his assertion
> And may appear so when the dog-star rages –
> And he who understands it would be able
> To add a story to the Tower of Babel
> (*Don Juan*, 'Dedication', verse iv, 1819)

and:

> A drowsy, frowzy poem called the "Excursion"
> Writ in a manner which is my aversion
> (*Don Juan*, Canto 3, verse xciv, 1821).

Most critics agree with Byron, many noting that this work degenerates into abstraction and, in the absence of the concrete imagery that characterises his best poems, becomes ponderous and vague.

This poem failed to fire the imagination as Wordsworth intended it to, being hampered by an unsustainable philosophical viewpoint. Much of *The Excursion* concerns how it is possible to live as a being alienated from nature rather than as an organism embedded in it. If we are estranged from the natural world, then we are estranged from the stimulation that is vital for an imaginative life, and often troubled by a general malaise that prevents us from exploring our true humanity.

Shelley found that Wordsworth's later work betrayed the wonder of his earlier poetry. In his sonnet 'To Wordsworth' he wrote:

> Thou wert as a lone star, whose light did shine …
> Thou hast like to a rock-built refuge stood
> Above the blind a battling multitude:
> In honoured poverty thy voice did weave
> Songs consecrate to truth and liberty, –
> Deserting these, thou leavest me to grieve,
> Thus having been, that thou shouldst cease to be.
> (Abrams 1979, p.665)

Thomas McFarland, in 1992, presented a harsh criticism:

> The visionary splendour faded, Coleridge no longer there to spur him and guide him, rigidity in politics and religion deadening him, still he wrote. And he irritates; for it was only by the presence of his unique intensity that he was a great poet, and that intensity gone, he scarcely deserved the name of poet at all. (McFarland, p.97)

Others, however, were less concerned by Wordsworth's decline, and placed much more emphasis on the achievements of his finest poetry. **John Stuart Mill**, the nineteenth-century philosopher who was an exponent of a utilitarian society (his 'greatest happiness principle' held that one must always act to produce the greatest happiness for the greatest number of people) lauded Wordsworth's work. He found Wordsworth's poems to be a 'perennial source of happiness' that:

> seemed to draw from a source of inward joy, of sympathetic and imaginative pleasure, which could be shared in by all human beings; which had no connexion with struggle or imperfection ... [t]here was real, permanent happiness in tranquil contemplation. (Mill 1965, p.91)

Mill, then, found in Wordsworth an expression of the source of human vitality – our relationship with nature.

The nineteenth-century poet and critic **Matthew Arnold** also praised Wordsworth: '[his] performance in poetry is on the whole, in power, in interest, in the qualities which give enduring freshness' (Arnold 1949, pp.337–8). He is the most discerning of critics, though, and attempts an analysis of why Wordsworth had not, among his contemporaries, achieved his rightful 'place among the poets' (p.338). He proposes that what is at the heart of the criticism is that among the seven volumes of his works there are 'pieces of high merit ... mingled with a mass of pieces very inferior to them; so inferior ... that it seems wonderful how the same poet should have produced both' (p.338). The crux of the problem as Arnold sees it is that:

> work altogether inferior, work quite uninspired, flat and dull, is produced by him with evident unconsciousness of its defects ... and he presents it to us with the same faith and seriousness as his best work ... the impression made by one of his fine pieces is too often dulled and spoiled by a very inferior piece coming after it. (pp.338–9)

Arnold proposes that the body of Wordsworth's work be dissected and 'relieved of a great deal of the poetical baggage which now encumbers him' (p.339). Today, of course, we have the benefit of such a process through selected editions of his poetry, although critics still disagree on which poems to include in these selections.

Wordsworth's decline

No one is able to pinpoint with any certainty the reasons for the decline in Wordsworth's artistic powers. They certainly coincided with several occurrences:

- He became disenchanted with the conservative outcome of the French Revolution, which ended with a return to imperialism in the figure of Napoleon.
- His youthful political ideals and allegiances were revised in favour of a more conservative viewpoint.
- His sometime friend and critic, Coleridge, became increasingly unstable and emotional. It is well known that Coleridge experimented heavily with drugs that we would now class as illicit.
- His marriage to Mary Hutchinson had far-reaching consequences:
    - he became separated from his muse, his sister Dorothy, who was no longer his close companion
    - he found domestic life stifling
    - he had an urgent need to earn funds to maintain his household.

It is more than likely, though, that the sensibility and passion that allowed his art to flourish declined as he matured, and that the complete self-belief that was required to unflinchingly confront human limitations had waned. He also found that, in a society which rejected the idea of nature as something essential and immutable, he had no choice but to withdraw into self-absorption and domesticity. He came to realise that society as a whole, with all its imperfections, did not share his views about the importance of achieving harmony with nature.

Two interpretations

Texts are open to different interpretations, and this is especially true of poetry. As long as you can support a reading from the text with the evidence that is contained in the poem, several readings might be considered valid.

For example, if we look at an enigmatic poem such as **'Nutting'** (pp.75–6), two readings might be considered reasonable, both of which are discussed below.

Reading 1

In 'Nutting', Wordsworth uses a biblical analogy to represent the conflicting primary human emotions within us all.

The speaker sets out with his nutting hook (used to pull down tree branches) on a 'heavenly' day (l.2). This image is heavy with biblical associations, as the references to the perfection of the Garden of Eden are clear.

There is a suggestion that the speaker is in 'disguise' (l.7) as a beggar, suggesting that he is misrepresenting himself by appearing 'More ragged than need was' (l.12). We must ask ourselves why he stresses this point, and what relevance it has to the rest of the poem. 'Motley accoutrements' (l.9) has wider literary reference, as clowns and jesters often wear such parti-coloured costumes. The suggestion is that he does not want to be recognised. Is his conduct spontaneous or pre-planned, then?

The speaker reaches a primeval 'nook' (l.14) which is, significantly, 'Unvisited' (l.15). The following description is of a paradisiacal scene: 'the hazels rose/Tall and erect, with milk-white clusters hung' (ll.17–18). The biblical images of an unspoiled paradise are reinforced by the emphasis on 'A virgin scene!' (l.19).

The speaker revels in the landscape's unblemished beauty, but the images also reflect a disturbing overlay of sensuality. The words 'Voluptuous' (l.22) and 'banquet' (l.23) suggest sensual excess or extravagance, giving the speaker's position 'Among the flowers, and with the flowers' (l.24) a more loaded meaning. These overripe, sexualised images of nature contrast markedly with the preceding chasteness of the 'virgin scene' and the prior references to paradise.

The speaker reaches a state of euphoria following a time of worry 'after long/And weary expectation' (ll.25–6). The poem intends to create a number of relations between God, humankind and nature, as the speaker gains a sense of belonging in the universe. God, who is immanent throughout his entire creation, affects the poet just as he affects everything else. The human spirit, like the spirit of God, is immanent in nature. The speaker is very much a part of this scene, rather than a mere observer: it is he who sees 'the sparkling foam/And with [his] cheek on one of those green stones' (ll.32–3) reaches a 'Tribute to ease' (l.37) his spirit.

The ecstatic mood, though, is suddenly broken with 'Then up I rose' (l.40). There follows a frantic and wanton destruction of the paradise he has enjoyed. The language is graphic: 'crash', 'merciless ravage', 'Deformed and sullied' as he almost hysterically ruins the purity of the nook. The analogy with the destruction of paradise is clear. Just like Adam and Eve, he is at first 'Exulting' (l.49), but this is quickly followed by his feelings of a sharp 'sense of pain' (l.50) at the vandalism he has wrought. And nature sits in judgement on him with its 'silent trees and the intruding sky' (l.51).

Just what sparks this sudden urge to wreck perfection is uncertain. Certainly, there is a suggestion of possible sexual frustration as the speaker first indulges in the voluptuousness of the scene with a tactile response (ll.19–33). There are also the references to a 'suppression of the heart' (l.20) and 'The heart luxuriates with indifferent things' (l.38) that may well reflect sexual longing. The last three lines, which introduce a previously unmentioned 'dearest Maiden' (l.52), make more sense if we take this as a sensual reference. The 'gentleness of heart' (l.53) certainly is in direct contrast to the ending of the main body of the poem, which is forbidding and hostile. And what sort of a 'spirit' is it in the woods? This represents, perhaps, the immanence of God made manifest in nature; as such, it can be seen as an attempt to recast the initial biblical analogy of Eden in a pagan form that fully incorporates God within the natural world.

Reading 2

In 'Nutting' Wordsworth uses the natural environment to provide inspiration for the human imagination.

Wordsworth grounded his poetry in his own feelings, finding nature to be the prime source of the human imagination; and it is through the imagination that we can create a sense of belonging in the universe. In 'Nutting', Wordsworth shows how the imagination shapes our knowledge and our fears. The imagination, stimulated above all by the natural world, is the basis for reflecting on our humanity.

The speaker demonstrates varied states of mind. He starts off on a fine 'heavenly' (l.2) day swinging a satchel and a nutting hook in a jaunty gait 'Towards the distant woods' (l.6). The emphasis on distance shows that he has time to allow his imagination to work. He is dressed as a rustic in 'Beggar's weeds' (l.7) so that he will not ruin good clothes on 'thorns, and brakes, and brambles' (l.11). His ostensible purpose is to gather nuts, although this is only an excuse for the journey as there is no further reference to the actual harvesting of nuts. He refers to the fact that he was rather overdressed in his concealing outfit, 'More ragged than need was' (l.12), but does not explain why he should be wearing a 'disguise' (l.7).

Reaching a 'dear nook' (l.14) untouched by human activity, he uses this place to give his imagination full reign. Here 'not a broken bough/ Drooped with its withered leaves', but 'the hazels rose/Tall and erect, with milk-white clusters hung' (ll.17–18). This, he stresses is a 'virgin scene', a perfect environment where he can find repose and explore his emotions. Further, with physical connotations, he indulges his senses 'Among the flowers' (l.24), becoming a part of the scene rather than just an onlooker.

The shock of what follows, then, is even more startling. In line 40, after a caesura (a pause or break, created here by the full stop), the phrase 'Then up I rose' changes the tone completely from one of peace and restfulness to one of aggression and violence. The act of nutting ought to be a symbol of nature's bounty, but here the nutting hook becomes an instrument of destruction. This Edenic corner is wantonly destroyed by human anger and frustrated passion.

If we take as a premise Wordsworth's argument that poetry can 'change men's moral behavior' and that our habits and tales of distress can 'incorporate [themselves] with the blood and vital juices of our minds' (Johnston 1998, p.636), we might better understand the irrational vandalism that the speaker inflicts on a paradisiacal scene. In this way, Wordsworth declares poetry 'more socially effective than philosophy. Men will never be reasoned into good actions ... but they may be moved to them by powerful images' (Johnston, p.636). One such powerful image is the dragging 'to earth both branch and bough, with crash/And merciless ravage' (ll.41–2) that the speaker perpetrates on his pristine environment. The images of wanton destruction portrayed in 'Nutting' reflect this philosophical stance. Wordsworth concludes that we might become 'practically useful by informing ourselves to the means of turning them into a more beneficial course' (Johnston, p.636). The true feelings of the speaker, though, remain enigmatic apart from the naked aggression he displays. Wordsworth is possibly suggesting that his readers must learn to appreciate their interdependence with nature by reflecting on the totality of their experiences with it.

The poem ends with a contrast between the 'silent trees and the intruding sky' (l.51) that the speaker imagines as silently condemning his actions, and an idyllic scene of a maiden 'In gentleness of heart' (l.53) moving with an almost psychic awareness of a 'Spirit in the woods' (l.54). The speaker's imagination has clearly been stimulated by the natural setting, but only later does he come to realise that there are spiritual, as well as sensual, qualities inherent in the scene.

Summary

'Nutting' is a complex and enigmatic poem that is not easily analysed or explained. Clearly, several interpretations are possible and these two suggested readings, while defensible, are not exclusive.

No single reading of a poem is ever completely conclusive. The poet endeavours to suggest ideas and thoughts through poetic diction and allusion, but these do not come alive until the reader cooperates with the writer in interpreting them.

QUESTIONS & ANSWERS

This section focuses on your own analytical writing on the text, and gives you strategies for producing high quality responses in your coursework and exam essays.

Essay writing – an overview

An essay is a formal and serious piece of writing that presents your point of view on the text, usually in response to a given essay topic. Your 'point of view' in an essay is your interpretation of the meaning of the text's language, structure, characters, situations and events, supported by detailed analysis of textual evidence.

Analyse – don't summarise

In your essays it is important to avoid simply summarising what happens in a text:

- A **summary** is a description or paraphrase (retelling in different words) of the characters and events. For example: 'Macbeth has a horrifying vision of a dagger dripping with blood before he goes to murder King Duncan'.
- An **analysis** is an explanation of the real meaning or significance that lies 'beneath' the text's words (and images, for a film). For example: 'Macbeth's vision of a bloody dagger shows how deeply uneasy he is about the violent act he is contemplating – as well as his sense that supernatural forces are impelling him to act'.

A limited amount of summary is sometimes necessary to let your reader know which part of the text you wish to discuss. However, always keep this to a minimum and follow it immediately with your analysis (explanation) of what this part of the text is really telling us.

Plan your essay

Carefully plan your essay so that you have a clear idea of what you are going to say. The plan ensures that your ideas flow logically, that your argument remains consistent and that you stay on the topic. An essay plan should be a list of **brief dot points** – no more than half a page. The essay plan should include:

- your central argument or main contention – a concise statement (usually in a single sentence) of your overall response to the topic. See 'Analysing a sample topic' for guidelines on how to formulate a main contention.
- three or four dot points for each paragraph indicating the main idea and evidence/examples from the text. Note that in your essay you will need to *expand* on these points and *analyse* the evidence.

Structure your essay

An essay is a complete, self-contained piece of writing. It has a clear beginning (the introduction), middle (several body paragraphs) and end (the last paragraph or conclusion). It must also have a central argument that runs throughout, linking each paragraph to form a coherent whole.

See examples of introductions and conclusions in the 'Analysing a sample topic' and 'Sample answer' sections.

The introduction establishes your overall response to the topic. It includes your main contention and outlines the main evidence you will refer to in the course of the essay. Write your introduction *after* you have done a plan and *before* you write the rest of the essay.

The body paragraphs argue your case – they present evidence from the text and explain how this evidence supports your argument. Each body paragraph needs:

- a strong **topic sentence** (usually the first sentence) that states the main point being made in the paragraph
- **evidence** from the text, including some brief quotations

- **analysis** of the textual evidence explaining its significance and **explanation** of how it supports your argument
- **links back to the topic** in one or more statements, usually towards the end of the paragraph.

Connect the body paragraphs so that your discussion flows smoothly. Use some linking words and phrases like 'similarly' and 'on the other hand', though don't start every paragraph like this. Another strategy is to use a significant word from the last sentence of one paragraph in the first sentence of the next.

Use key terms from the topic – or synonyms for them – throughout, so the relevance of your discussion to the topic is always clear.

The conclusion ties everything together and finishes the essay. It includes strong statements that emphasise your central argument and provide a clear response to the topic.

Avoid simply restating the points made earlier in the essay – this will end on a very flat note and imply that you have run out of ideas and vocabulary. The conclusion is meant to be a logical extension of what you have written, not just a repetition or summary of it. Writing an effective conclusion can be a challenge. Try using these tips:

- Start by linking back to the final sentence of the second-last paragraph – this helps your writing to 'flow', rather than just leaping back to your main contention straight away.
- Use synonyms and expressions with equivalent meanings to vary your vocabulary. This allows you to reinforce your line of argument without being repetitive.
- When planning your essay, think of one or two broad statements or observations about the text's wider meaning. These should be related to the topic and your overall argument. Keep them for the conclusion, since they will give you something 'new' to say but still follow logically from your discussion. The introduction will be focused on the topic, but the conclusion can present a wider view of the text.

Essay topics

1 "I was a traveller then upon the moor".
'The use of first-person narration allows Wordsworth to show a speaker's deeply personal involvement.' Do you agree?

2 'Wordsworth shows us that the contemplation of nature can be a way of lightening feelings of melancholy and despondence.' Discuss.

3 Wordsworth refers to "a higher power than Fancy". How does he demonstrate the dynamic power of the imagination in his poems?

4 "Ships, towers, domes, theatres, and temples lie/Open unto the fields".
'Wordsworth successfully marries the contrasting ideas of unfettered nature and the edifices we have constructed.' Discuss.

5 "Behold her, single in the field/Yon solitary highland lass".
'Wordsworth uses varied images of simple rustics to highlight the heroic in ordinary human life.' Discuss.

6 'Wordsworth demonstrates that a contemplation of nature brings an understanding of human endeavour.' Discuss.

7 "Their graves are green, they may be seen/The little maid replied".
Discuss the creative role that children play in Wordsworth's poetry.

8 "O mercy! To myself I cried/If Lucy should be dead".
What is Wordsworth's purpose in highlighting sudden moods of intense fear?

9 'Wordsworth shows an awareness of a spiritual reality both in and beyond the natural world.' Discuss.

10 "My Lucy's race was run".
'While much of his poetry celebrates the joys of human life, Wordsworth also focuses on human grief and loss.' Discuss.

Analysing a sample topic

"I was a traveller then upon the moor". 'The use of first-person narration allows Wordsworth to show a speaker's deeply personal involvement.' Do you agree?

The topic asks you to explore Wordsworth's use of a first-person speaker and how that device shows the speaker's personal involvement. There are two aspects: a) a demonstration of your knowledge of how and why the poet uses first-person narration; and b) a contention linking the speaker's personal involvement with his subject matter.

- Many topics include several parts and all must be examined. Here the key words are: **first-person narration** and his **deeply personal involvement**.
- When discussing first-person narration, it is important to note the distinction between the poet and the speaker. They are not necessarily one and the same even though Wordsworth often seems to be recording autobiographical incidents. You might make this clear in your introduction.

Sample introduction

> Wordsworth's first-person speakers bring to readers an awareness of the transforming power of the imagination. While the poet and the speaker are not synonymous, there is a deeply personal involvement that Wordsworth displays through his narration strategies. In contrast to omniscient narration, the use of first-person speakers allows Wordsworth to bring an immediacy to experiences that engage and involve readers. In this way Wordsworth is able to demonstrate one of the primary tenets of his poetry: the capacity to transform melancholy and sadness through recollection and reflection on personal experience. He does this by unfolding, and making personal, the intricate relationship between humanity and the natural environment.

First body paragraph

- Explain the role of the speaker in Wordsworth's poems. You might choose 'Resolution and Independence' as an example because it is the speaker who observes the leech-gatherer and is changed by the encounter. Briefly chart those changes. The speaker is despondent until he meets the old man who appears to represent the figure of a prophet.
- Incorporate the images of the seer/prophet.
- Discuss his role in the poem – how, by appearing to be part of nature, his simple endurance becomes a model of 'resolution and independence' for the speaker, whose life and mood are transformed. Be sure to include evidence to support your assertions.

Second body paragraph

- You might choose 'I Wandered Lonely as a Cloud' by way of contrast. Here it is nature, rather than another human being, that teaches the speaker the value of both nature and the faculty of memory.
- Discuss the way the imagery is important for the speaker's purpose.
- Show how important the idea of recollection is to show the speaker's 'deeply personal involvement'.

Third body paragraph

- For a third example you could select one of the long narrative poems such as 'Michael' or 'The Ruined Cottage' where the speaker records a story told by another person.
- Discuss how the speaker's role varies from that in the other examples.
- Show whether or not there is a 'deeply personal involvement' in these epic poems. This can be a point of comparison and contrast.
- Give evidence from the poem. You do not have to cover the entire poem, just be selective and keep to a discussion of the role of the speaker.

Conclusion

- Bring the discussion together by summing up the different ways Wordsworth uses the device of speaker. Reiterate that the persona is a device only and does not represent the poet's real voice or experiences.
- Finishing with an apt quotation is a useful ploy in drawing your discussion to a close.

Sample conclusion

> Wordsworth shows a deeply personal involvement in his poetry through the use of first-person narration strategies. While these vary from the overtly personal, such as in 'I Wandered Lonely as a Cloud', to complex narration strategies in 'The Ruined Cottage', his overall purpose is to show how the imagination can transform our experiences. First-person speakers have the effect of involving readers directly in both the joys and sadness of human existence. In this way, Wordsworth shows that recollection and meditation on our experiences can bring an unexpected release from melancholy and sorrow, that 'the fear that kills' can be dispelled through contemplation and 'the bliss of solitude'.

SAMPLE ANSWER

"My Lucy's race was run".
'While much of his poetry celebrates the joys of human life, Wordsworth also focuses on human grief and loss.' Discuss.

Through images and descriptions of the natural world, Wordsworth celebrates the joys of human life, but he is always mindful of the personal elements of grief and loss. By using nature, and men and women within nature, as the inspiration for his imagination, Wordsworth is able to portray a range of human emotions. Often these are most vivid for his speakers when they use memory as a guide for re-ordering their own experiences; thus, Wordsworth is able to explore what moves all of us to both joy and grief.

The complexity of Wordsworth's poetic vision is apparent when he uses recollections of experiences in the natural world to explore feelings of happiness as well as sorrow. In 'I Wandered Lonely as a Cloud', the speaker reflects on the delight of a moment when he first saw a mass display of daffodils. At the time, the sight of this sea of gold had little effect but later when, in contemplation, his mind returns to the sight, his imagination imbues the simple scene with a new and greater significance. The daffodils become personified as a 'crowd' that moves in unison, 'fluttering and dancing in the breeze'. The speaker had not immediately realised the 'wealth' of 'pleasure' that he would later gain from the massed flowers, but when he recalls them in repose, that experience is transposed into an almost spiritual understanding of the joy that nature brings to human life.

In a natural extension of his poetic sensibility, Wordsworth is able to contrast this joy of life in the natural world with a sense of grief and loss. In 'Three years she grew', the speaker imagines his daughter as a child, whom a personified nature claims, being protected by 'earth and heaven'. She is nurtured to run freely 'across the lawn/Or up the mountain springs', to be (with an apt simile) 'as sportive as' a 'fawn', to have a vital energy and the capacity for an imaginative appreciation of her world. Thus, she is not just passively moulded but a living, breathing being who will develop surrounded by happiness: 'delight' and 'beauty … shall pass into her face'. This is how the speaker imagines his daughter growing to maturity. There is, however, a dramatic inversion in the final stanza with a reversal of the speaker's joyous vision giving way to the reality that Lucy has died. She is now just a 'memory', yet his grief and loss, evident in the mournful closing line 'And never more will be', are tempered by the knowledge that life and death are, inevitably, creative opposites.

While Wordsworth is able to portray a universal truth about life and death with the memory of Lucy, he is acutely aware of the pain and grief of human loss. In 'The Thorn', his speaker creates a sense of primeval nature through a sustained description of an aged 'thorn' tree. It is 'a mass of knotted joints' with the appearance of a 'stone'; it has remained immovable on the side of a mountain path since time immemorial. Its age and unattractiveness are then starkly contrasted with 'a fresh and lovely sight/A beauteous heap' in a dell where multicoloured moss grows over a mound of earth the size of 'an infant's grave'. This melancholy image of a child's death marries with the prior image of the 'forlorn' thorn tree.

Overseeing the whole, though, is a woman strikingly dressed in a 'scarlet cloak'. Her sudden appearance in stanza six makes her displays of misery and woe all the more arresting. She has been there, so legend suggests, for so long, always chanting a 'doleful' refrain, that she now seems to have become transmuted into a part of the natural scene. The speaker recounts how the woman, 'Martha Ray', was jilted by her lover on the eve of her wedding. She had then suffered a double loss with the subsequent death of her child – whether by her own hand or not remains a mystery. She becomes an image of overt grief and loss that can never be reconciled.

Wordsworth balances his observations of the world with his desire to imaginatively re-shape and re-create in poetry the objects observed. He achieves this through presenting his readers with first-person narrators who experience both the joys of life and the pain of grief and loss. For many of his speakers, ordinary life experiences later provide moments of spiritual revelation as they recall significant instances of awareness that bring delight or comfort. Wordsworth shows the imaginative power that solitude brings, away from the noise and strife of everyday life. Imagination and memory, he suggests, are powerful tools that present the possibility of transcending loss and allow us to gain a more complete understanding and acceptance of human life.

REFERENCES & READING

Text

Wordsworth, W 2004, *Selected Poems*, ed. Stephen Gill, Penguin, London.

Although this edition is widely available, it uses early versions of the poems rather than the more accepted, later revisions; for these later versions see the *Norton Anthology* (1979) below.

References

Abrams, MH 1971 (1957), *A Glossary of Literary Terms*, Holt, Rinehart and Winston, New York.

Abrams, MH et al. 1979, *The Norton Anthology of English Literature, Vol. II*, 4th Edition, Norton, New York.

Arnold, M 1949, *The Essential Matthew Arnold*, ed. Lionel Trilling, Viking Press, London.

Johnston, K R 1998, *The Hidden Wordsworth: Poet, Lover, Spy*, Norton, New York.

McFarland, T 1992, 'Wordsworth's Dessication', *William Wordsworth: Intensity and Achievement*, Clarendon Press, Oxford.

Mill, JS 1965, *Essential Works of John Stuart Mill*, ed. Max Lerner, Bantam Books, New York.

Plath, S 1998 (1985), *Selected Poems*, Faber & Faber, London.

Stevens, W 1972 (1967), *The Palm at the End of the Mind*, ed. Holly Stevens, Vintage Books, New York.

Wordsworth, W 1994, *Selected Poems*, ed. John O. Hayden, Penguin, London.

—2007, *The Complete Poetical Works of William Wordsworth*, Vols. 1 & 2, ed. John Morley, Kessinger Publishing.

APPENDIX: THREE POEMS

Three poems are included here for ease of reference. The versions of 'I Wandered Lonely as a Cloud' and 'Strange Fits of Passion Have I known' are revised – and more widely accepted – versions of those included in the *Selected Poems*. 'Steamboats, Viaducts, and Railways' is omitted from the *Selected Poems* but is discussed briefly in this guide.

I Wandered Lonely as a Cloud

I wandered lonely as a cloud
That floats on high o'er vales and hills,
When all at once I saw a crowd,
A host, of golden daffodils;
Beside the lake, beneath the trees,
Fluttering and dancing in thc breeze.

Continuous as the stars that shine
And twinkle on the milky way,
They stretched in never-ending line
Along the margin of a bay:
Ten thousand saw I at a glance,
Tossing their heads in sprightly dance.

The waves beside them danced; but they
Outdid the sparkling waves in glee;
A poet could not but be gay,
In such a jocund company;
I gazed—and gazed—but little thought
What wealth the show to me had brought:

For oft, when on my couch I lie
In vacant or in pensive mood,
They flash upon that inward eye
Which is the bliss of solitude;
And then my heart with pleasure fills,
And dances with the daffodils.

Steamboats, Viaducts, and Railways

Motions and Means, on land and sea at war
With old poetic feeling, not for this,
Shall ye, by Poets even, be judged amiss!
Nor shall your presence, howsoe'er it mar
The loveliness of Nature, prove a bar
To the Mind's gaining that prophetic sense
Of future change, that point of vision, whence
May be discovered what in soul ye are.
In spite of all that beauty may disown
In your harsh features, Nature doth embrace
Her lawful offspring in Man's art; and Time,
Pleased with your triumphs o'er his brother Space,
Accepts from your bold hands the proffered crown
Of hope, and smiles on you with cheer sublime.

Strange Fits of Passion Have I Known

Strange fits of passion have I known:
And I will dare to tell,
But in the Lover's ear alone,
What once to me befell.

When she I loved looked every day
Fresh as a rose in June,
I to her cottage bent my way,
Beneath an evening moon.

Upon the moon I fixed my eye,
All over the wide lea;
With quickening pace my horse drew nigh
Those paths so dear to me.

And now we reached the orchard plot;
And, as we climbed the hill,
The sinking moon to Lucy's cot
Came near, and nearer still.

In one of those sweet dreams I slept,
Kind Nature's gentlest Boon!
And all the while my eyes I kept
On the descending moon.

My horse moved on; hoof after hoof
He raised, and never stopped:
When down behind the cottage roof,
At once, the bright moon dropped.

What fond and wayward thoughts will slide
Into a Lover's head!
'O mercy!' to myself I cried,
'If Lucy should be dead!'

INDEX OF POEMS